# Jean Arthur

# Jean Arthur

## A Biofilmography

Jerry Vermilye

authorHOUSE®

*AuthorHouse™*
*1663 Liberty Drive*
*Bloomington, IN 47403*
*www.authorhouse.com*
*Phone: 1-800-839-8640*

*Published by AuthorHouse    05/29/2012*

*ISBN: 978-1-4670-4327-4 (sc)*
*ISBN: 978-1-4670-4326-7 (e)*

*Library of Congress Control Number: 2011917720*

## Also by Jerry Vermilye

Burt Lancaster
Bette Davis
Cary Grant
Barbara Stanwyck
Ida Lupino
The Great British Films
The Films of Charles Bronson
The Films of the Thirties
The Films of the Twenties

More Films of the Thirties
The Complete Films of Laurence Olivier
Great Italian Films
The Complete Films of Audrey Hepburn
Ingmar Bergman: His Life and Films
Buster Crabbe: A Bio-Filmography
The Boothbay Playhouse
500 Best British and Foreign Films to
Buy, Rent or Videotape (editor)

*And with Mark Ricci*
The Films of Elizabeth Taylor

. . . . . . . . . . . . . . . . . . . . . . . . . . . . . . . . . . . . . . . . . . . . . .

For
Mary Huntington
and
Pond House
where this book
was written

. . . . . . . . . . . . . . . . . . . . . . . . . . . . . . . . . . . . . . . . . . . . . .

# ACKNOWLEDGMENTS

The author wishes to express his gratitude to the following for giving so generously of their time and/or erudition to supply information, research material and pictorial images—or for offering editorial advice, manuscript assistance and a congenial work environment: Judy and Paul Caputo, Jeff Carrier, Tom Cavanaugh, Bob Finn, Joe Frazzetta, Barry Gillam, Peter J. Hawke, Mary Huntington, Kenneth G. Lawrence, Maeve McGuire, Romano Tozzi, Allan Turner and Elizabeth Turner-Hall.

*Jerry Vermilye*

And a salute to all of the anonymous news, still and portrait photographers whose artistry illustrates these pages, as well as to the movie companies and releasing organizations who gave us the films of Jean Arthur: Anchor Film Distributors, Approved Pictures, Artclass Pictures, Buster Keaton Productions, Clifford S. Elfelt Productions, Columbia Pictures, Davis Distributing Division, Film Booking Offices of America (F.B.O.), First National Pictures, Fox Film Corp., Goodwill Pictures, Gotham Productions, Harry Garson Productions, Independent Pictures, Jess Smith Productions, Lumas Film Corp., Metro-Goldwyn-Mayer, Monty Banks Enterprises, Paramount Pictures, RKO Radio Pictures, Tiffany Productions, 20th Century-Fox, United Artists, Universal Pictures, Warner Bros. and Weiss Brothers.

# CONTENTS

# PREFACE

Perhaps it's not surprising that, 59 years after the release of her last film, not everyone knows who Jean Arthur was. But those interested in classic movies from Hollywood's "golden age" will be acquainted with such Arthur pictures as *Mr. Deeds Goes to Town, You Can't Take It With You, Mr. Smith Goes to Washington, The More the Merrier* and, of course, *Shane.* Turner Classic Movies (TCM) has helped preserve her screen image on cable television, and a number of her films are now available on DVD. But, characteristic of a star who closely guarded her privacy, unlike Greta Garbo, there's no legendary persona to consider. Lacking the glamorous allure of a Garbo, the somewhat more earthbound Arthur's legacy centers mainly on images of a warm and witty blonde, whose unique charm centered on her voice. That fetchingly odd voice with its unexpected breaks and childish tones—querulous at times—is what most people remember.

Jean Arthur's movie career spanned exactly 30 years and encompassed 89 pictures, including many long-forgotten silents and B-Westerns. Her unusual and considerable talents remain an indelible part of film history, and this illustrated celebration of that career is offered in tribute to her art.

# THE BIOGRAPHY

*"I guess I became an actress because I didn't want to be myself."*
*—Jean Arthur (1972)*

She was born Gladys Georgianna Greene on October 17, 1900, a year destined to become obscured by an obsessive personal desire to bury the truth of her origins. The day and month of her birth would remain as established, but the year an adult Gladys Greene would insist on claiming as her own became 1908. And she would strenuously object to anyone's efforts to dispute that date.

Her Vermont-born father had left home at 18 to head West and become a cowboy. While working as a ranch hand in the 1880s, he'd found time to develop an interest in painting and photography, inspired by the landscapes of Montana, where he met his future wife. Before settling in upstate Plattsburgh, New York, where Gladys was born, the Greenes had also lived in North Dakota and Florida. Gladys was the first daughter born to Hubert Sidney Greene and Johannah (known as "Hannah") Augusta Nelson Greene, already the parents of sons Don (born 1890), Robert (1892) and Albert (1894). In Plattsburgh, where they lived a middle-class life in a rented house, her father modestly supported his family as a photographer employed by the George T. Woodward studio. Being a girl and the youngest child by six years, Gladys assuaged her loneliness with her large collection of dolls, for which she made clothing. But envy of her three older brothers and their adventurous pursuits eventually motivated her to such boyish games as Cowboys and Indians. As she later elucidated: "I felt cheated, frustrated. I became a tomboy in self-defense. I decided I was going to do things that were exciting, or at least interesting."

The family was not to remain settled in Plattsburgh; Hubert Greene's work occasioned frequent moves ranging from New England to Florida, with the result that young Gladys's schooling depended on their living situation. For a child who was already both lonely and unsure of herself, this only increased her introversion. She was not invited to children's parties and never belonged to any kind of youthful sisterhood. In middle age, she would later admit: "I've never had a single close, intimate girl friend in all my life. I never had a chum to whom I could confide my secrets. I suppose that accounts for the fact that now it is so painfully difficult for me to open my heart and confide in people who are, so often, almost strangers. You have to learn so very young to open your heart."

Enjoying little rapport with her mother and generally ignored by her brothers, Gladys adored her father, whose approval she found less problematic. While Hannah Greene embraced Christian Science and attained to high moral values, Hubert enjoyed alcohol and especially loved painting. In fact, the couple had little in common.

Gladys Greene at seven, as photographed by her father
(author's collection).

By 1908, the Greenes were living in Portland, Maine, where Hubert now managed a thriving portrait gallery called the Lamson Studio. The following year, when the family was spending time in Jacksonville, Florida, Hubert Greene suddenly deserted them. It was particularly devastating for Gladys, who felt abandoned by the parent she loved most, and whose affection had always been unconditional. The elder Greene would be back with his family in Portland in 1910, but his pattern of departures without explanation would persist.

To establish a more secure financial existence, Hannah Greene was forced to open a boarding house in Portland, where 11-year-old Gladys helped with the housekeeping chores. As a sixth-grader at Portland North School, she scored respectable grades that September of 1912, only to have her young life uprooted a month later when the Greenes moved to Jacksonville. Unable to maintain a photography business of his own, Hubert Greene now went back to work for George T. Woodward, who had relocated his studio in Florida.

If young Gladys had felt lonely in her pre-adolescence, her lot was not soon to improve. In their Jacksonville home, Hannah and Hubert Greene took to living separate lives in different parts of the same big house. And Gladys' brothers left home to pursue their own lives: Albert returned to Portland to pursue photography; Bob became a traveling salesman; and Don, who shared his father's fondness for the bottle, temporarily drifted into a life of obscurity.

In 1913, Gladys Greene found an unexpected role model when her Aunt Pearl Nelson, her mother's half-sister and an extroverted, charismatic schoolteacher, elected to move from Billings, Montana, to Jacksonville. Continuing her career in Florida, Pearl would live with Hannah and offer her support through an ever-worsening marriage. Aunt Pearl brought an appreciation of the arts and culture into Gladys' lonely life.

Unfortunately, this stimulating new family influence was not to last long. With domestic problems further affecting the Greene marriage, Gladys was now sent away to live with her father's parents in Schenectady, New York, where she resumed her fitful education in the autumn of 1914 at Howe Elementary School. Although known to her classmates as a loner, Gladys did well academically. A Schenectady neighbor later recalled her as "a very timid girl" who "kept to herself."

Amid the summer of 1915, Gladys' young life took a more exciting change altogether when Hubert Greene went to work for the successful New York City photographer Ira L. Hill at his Fifth Avenue studio. This promising position led to a new reconciliation of her parents that took them to living quarters in the Washington Heights section of upper Manhattan at 573 West 159th Street, a stone's throw from the picturesque Hudson River. An even more exciting part of their new neighborhood was the Audubon Theater, a vaudeville/movie venue that showed, for 10¢ a clip, the celluloid efforts of such Fox Film Corp. favorites as Theda Bara, Tom Mix and William Farnum. It was about this time that our Gladys also developed an appreciation of another "Gladys," better known to filmgoers as Mary Pickford, whose original surname was "Smith." With their promise of romance, adventure and excitement, the movies held a natural fascination and escape for a shy youngster like Gladys Greene, who could scarcely then imagine where life would take *her* a decade later.

That autumn, Gladys attended Fort Washington High School, where she mastered secretarial skills and gained an interest in romance languages. And, while her peers seemed more concerned with a future of finding husbands and becoming homemakers, Gladys knew that "I would never have become just a wife. I would have felt stifled with only housework to do." With thoughts of forging a career for herself, she entertained notions of teaching language, or working for a publishing company.

What was later referred to as "a change in family circumstances" interrupted those ideas of higher employment. Apparently, Hubert Greene's latest employment failed to work out, forcing Gladys to drop out of school in her junior year to help support the family. Proficient in shorthand, she now brought her secretarial training to use with a stenographer's position in downtown Bond Street. By the end of World War I in 1918, Gladys was living alone with her mother in the 159th Street apartment, for Hubert Greene had characteristically disappeared again. They were joined there by Gladys' brother Bob, following war service. Unfortunately, Albert Greene had succumbed to battle injuries.

By now, 18-year-old Gladys had developed into an attractive, blue-eyed brunette, maintaining her hair in a fashionably short bob and standing a petite five-foot-three. Her comely appearance would soon lead her into a lucrative modeling career. How this all came about remains somewhat cloudy. Most likely her father's professional connections had something to do with it, although years later she would relate the tale of accompanying a friend who was posing for a commercial photographer. "They asked me whether I would care to pose for girls' hats," she explained, "and with some diffidence I consented."

Commercial modeling, of course, held a monetary lure: at $5.00 a session, there were sometimes several sessions a day, as the reserved young woman became better known in the business. Perhaps her most celebrated employer at this time was the popular magazine illustrator Howard Chandler Christy, for whom she modeled at the Hotel des Artistes. By 1920, Gladys was also sitting for Alfred Cheney Johnston, a photographer known for his erotic, but artfully draped portraits of *Ziegfeld Follies* girls. Another of Johnston's models, with whom Gladys frequently came into contact, was an ambitious young Canadian named Norma Shearer, who soon gained fame in the Springfield Tires advertisements as "Miss Lotta Miles."

"Norma Shearer gained my wholehearted admiration for her business ability," her modeling colleague later remembered. "She made people realize her time was valuable. She was always prompt herself, and therefore got promptness and attention in return."

Shearer's perseverance began to get her roles in motion pictures shot in the East, and by 1923 was signed to a Hollywood contract. Despite her less forceful personality, Gladys was about to follow a similar path. The same year that took Shearer to the West Coast studios of Metro Pictures saw the shy Ms. Greene screen-tested by the New York division of Fox Films. This was part of a collaboration between Hollywood's William Fox and a group of Manhattan's top artists to develop new female stars for the screen, and Gladys Greene photographed impressively enough to secure herself a one-year movie contract. At 22, in the company of her mother, she boarded a train for California. With no assurance of her future, Gladys Greene could only have been inspired by the budding career of Norma Shearer, and more than a little bit frightened.

When it was suggested to Gladys that she choose a new name for motion pictures, she turned to her literary heroes, deriving "Arthur" from England's fabled King and "Jean" from the original French spelling of Joan of Arc. Fox immediately began to publicize the rechristened "Jean Arthur," with the result that she became the cover girl on *Movie Weekly* for September 8, 1923. Posed on a chair, with one shapely leg exposed, Fox's new starlet sported a sleeveless, low-bodiced mini-frock and a friendly smile. The studio now set out to promote her as a future star, with the sort of publicity hype that only a gullible fan-public could buy. Jean Arthur was thus described in Fox press kits as "one of the most beautiful leading women in motion pictures, whose charm and histrionic ability will win her thousands of new admirers."

It was an era in which the Hollywood studios churned out two-reel shorts (running approximately 20 minutes) to supplement their feature-length pictures, and Arthur's screen debut was in just such a featurette, a comedy called *Somebody Lied* that paired her with future Westerns star Ken Maynard.

Quickly produced in the summer of 1923, it was followed closely by the John Gilbert feature *Cameo Kirby*, in which Arthur wore period costumes and played a friend of the heroine (Gertrude Olmstead). It was a small role requiring little but girlish charm, under the direction of John Ford.

Having thus become familiar with the basic requirements of motion-picture acting, and gaining self-confidence with Fox's star-making build-up, Arthur now took on the lead in *The Temple of Venus*. This was a loosely structured story of little substance that served chiefly to showcase the "1,000 West Coast Beauties" that the release would eventually publicize as its big attraction. With Henry Otto directing, shooting began off the coast of Santa Barbara on Santa Cruz Island, and she began her new assignment with proud expectations and some trepidation. But Arthur found no rapport with director Otto, and her efforts to express what he wanted failed to materialize, despite a prolonged rehearsal period. Looking back on the experience, she would later analyze her inability to respond: "There wasn't a spark from within. I was acting like a mechanical doll personality."

After several days of shooting, Otto finally took her aside, explained that she was inadequate to the task and would be replaced by the more seasoned, 19-year-old Mary Philbin.

JA standing at right center in The Temple of Venus
(Fox Film Corp., 1923).

Jean Arthur was devastated. Years later, she could look back objectively on the crushing experience:

"... that is where and why I developed the most beautiful inferiority complex you've ever seen. Without any experience at all, I was cast in a starring role and expected to turn in a highly dramatic performance.

"After I finally got home, and sobbed out my failure to my mother, I didn't go near the studio for days. I was too ashamed and embarrassed . . . even to show my face."

That October saw the successive release of *Somebody Lied, Cameo Kirby* and *The Temple of Venus*, in which some usable early footage left her an unbilled extra among the bathing beauties. Perhaps there was a degree of poetic justice in the latter's negative critical reception. Nor did the reviewers have any kind words for Mary Philbin's performance.

After her disheartening experience with *The Temple of Venus*, Jean Arthur had wanted to return to New York. But Hannah Greene persuaded her to stay and fulfill her Fox contract, which consisted of the comedy short *Spring Fever*, opposite Al St. John, and a pair of comic two-reelers on loan-out to Universal, *Case Dismissed* and *The Powerful Eye*, both released in the spring of 1924. *Case Dismissed* cast her opposite Slim Summerville and moved *Motion Picture News* to call Arthur "a pretty girl with a personality that registers on the screen."

With her contractual obligations to Fox completed, she sought work as a free-lance player. Not yet an accomplished actress, she nevertheless enjoyed the assignments she was able to get, low-paying though they might be. She even worked gratis on one 18-hour shift for a film promoting a new nightclub, in the vain hope that it might lead to something better.

Hannah Greene's dressmaking skills helped support them during this slack period until Arthur learned of a low-budget series of Westerns to be produced by the modest Action Pictures Corporation. Its enterprising chief, Lester F. Scott, Jr., had a plan: hire three daredevil-riding cowboys and give them colorful new monikers. Thus, rodeo champ Jay Wilsey became "Buffalo Bill Jr.," Kent Sanderson assumed the screen name "Buddy Roosevelt" and Floyd T. Alderson traded that in for the more catchy "Wally Wales." Jean Arthur, despite her six unimpressive motion picture appearances to date, was almost equally unknown when she signed on to be the trio's spunky leading lady in these cheaply-made outdoor pictures, largely shot on desert locations under uncomfortable working conditions. The pay was small and the movie titles as forgettably generic as *Fast and Fearless, Tearin' Loose* and *The Roaring Rider*. There were an even dozen of them, released from 1924 to 1926, and in among these hard-riding, gun-slinging Westerns, Jean Arthur managed to secure work in a number of other pictures of similar bent. If nothing else, they gave the young actress experience and a degree of self-assurance. Many years later, director Richard Thorpe fondly recalled working with the "beautiful, charming" Arthur, and admiring her willingness to put up with such rugged film shoots with "the boys."

She also gained riding skills on these B-Westerns, inspiring *Motion Picture News* to report her in *The Hurricane Horseman* (1925) "not only a pretty heroine, but a worthy match for 'her man' when it comes to a question of daring equine stunts." That publication also remarked on Arthur's "very sweet and winning heroine" in *The Fighting Cheat*. These unpretentious little time-passers were especially popular in the grassroots communities of America's heartland.

Amid this period, Arthur played an uncredited bit as a receptionist in Buster Keaton's prestigious comedy *Seven Chances* (1925), a co-ed in *The College Boob* (1926), and bigger roles in a pair of comedic two-reelers back at Fox: *Eight-Cylinder Bull* and *The Mad Racer*. There were also stints as leading lady to the popular Western star Tom Tyler in *Born to Battle* and *The Cowboy Cop* (both 1926, Arthur's busiest year with 13 films released).

A decade later, Jean Arthur expressed her dissatisfactions with her career at this point: "First I played ingénues and Western heroines; then I played Western heroines and ingénues. That diet of roles became as monotonous as a diet of spinach. The studios wouldn't trust me with any other kind of role, because I had no experience in any other kind. And I didn't see how I was ever going to acquire any other experience if I couldn't get any other kind of role. It was a vicious circle."

*The Block Signal*, her final 1926 release, at least took her away from Westerns with its melodramatic railroad yarn, as did *The College Boob*, a trendy football comedy for FBO Pictures. Her next two were for the "poverty row" Tiffany Productions: *Husband Hunters*, as a naïve, aspiring chorus girl; and *The Broken Gate*, in which she played a collegian with romantic problems. Both were released in 1927, as were the last of her two-reel comedies: *Hello! LaFayette!* (aka *Lafayette, Where Are We?*), an additional Fox short, and *Bigger and Better Blondes*, a Charley Chase featurette made for the Hal Roach Studio. At Pathé that year, Arthur was the beleaguered heroine in her only serial, *The Masked Menace*, a minor 10-episode thriller opposite Larry Kent.

Chaplinesque comedian Monty Banks, who had his own production company, then engaged Arthur as his leading lady for a pair of 1927 comedies entitled *Horse Shoes* and *Flying Luck*. And then she landed a more important assignment when director Richard Wallace insisted on engaging her, over the protestations of First National executives, for the female lead opposite popular Jack Mulhall in *The Poor Nut*. It was the motion picture that not only showcased the actress to her widest audience, but also brought her her first personal notice in *The New York Times*, which lauded "the appeal of Jean Arthur."

William Courtwright, Charlie Murray and JA in The Poor Nut
(First National Pictures, 1927).

While many an aspiring Hollywood starlet would have been glad to be working in the movies at all, much less in leading roles, Jean Arthur was far from content with her modest success. It was a major issue of disagreement between her and Hannah Greene: "My mother says I'm ungrateful because I'm not satisfied. She says thousands of girls would be glad to get the parts I've had . . . leading lady to slapstick comedians, leading lady to cowboys in Westerns, leading lady in independents." Indeed, what she wanted above all was to be taken seriously as an *actress*. Her hopes would be raised when she tested for better roles at the major studios, only to be let down again when she failed to get them.

For FBO Pictures, she played a Southern country girl with big-city social ambitions in *Wallflowers* (1928). And at MGM she was called in to test for a William Haines movie, which she lost to another actress. However, when she took that test to the people at Paramount, they were sufficiently impressed to sign her for the Richard Dix baseball picture *Warming Up*. With Arthur in a smallish ingénue part, this rather ordinary silent was quickly augmented, prior to its midsummer 1928 release, with a musical score and synchronized sound effects to match the then-revolutionary technical changes that were unsettling most of Hollywood's stars and producers. *Warming Up* was thus misleadingly sold to the public as Paramount's first sound picture, despite the fact that it didn't feature dialogue. Nevertheless, its innovational aspects, promoted with "Hear what you see!" advertising insured its popularity. *Variety* thought little of its screenplay, but (while confusing her name) opined "Dix and June Arthur are splendid."

JA and Richard Dix in Warming Up
(Paramount Pictures, 1928).

The success of *Warming Up* inspired Paramount to sign her to a three-year contract beginning at $150. a week, a salary that not only drew Hubert Greene back to live with his wife and daughter, but brothers Don and Bob, as well.

Somewhere, in the early years of her movie career, Jean Arthur decided to reinvent her past, shaving some eight years from her life and obscuring details of her childhood. Thus anyone at the studio seeking to publicize her background was given 1908 as the year of her birth, and informed that she and Norma Shearer had arrived in Hollywood together as teenagers. In years to come, when rumors of a possible 1905 birth-date surfaced in interviews, Arthur would adamantly defend her claim to 1908. In an era when anyone in her mid-thirties might be considered "middle-aged," no movie star who valued her career could afford to be truthful about age. Of course, she was nearly 30 when she signed with Paramount, a fact known only to the Greene family, none of whom were about to jeopardize their meal ticket.

Perhaps this sudden regrouping of the clan, coincident with Arthur's elevated economic status, may have had something to do with her impetuous short-lived 1928 marriage, eloping to Santa Barbara with a young Jewish photographer named Julian Ancker. Arthur would recall his resemblance to Abraham Lincoln and that he "had a lot of good ideas." His religious background may have inspired in Arthur a welcome and rebellious alternative to Hannah Greene's strong affiliation with Christian Science. Whatever the motivation, the sudden union between Arthur and Ancker was annulled 24 hours later. The most popular explanation circulated was that the actress found that a clause in her Paramount contract didn't allow for marriage, so she'd had to decide between career and spouse. And, of course, the former won out. Reportedly, Ancker died soon thereafter, having suffered from sunstroke while fishing.

JA poses as Peter Pan for photographer Eugene Robert Richee
(Paramount Pictures, 1928).

In the late 1920s, Jean Arthur was much admired by a young Paramount executive named David O. Selznick, who appealed to her not for his looks but for his intellect. Her quirky shyness was quite the antithesis of his outspoken personality, and yet they shared enough in common to sustain a close friendship during a period when he was also dating his future wife, MGM boss Louis B. Mayer's daughter, Irene. Another intellectual figure that captured Arthur's interest at the time was Hollywood newcomer Oscar Levant, a songwriting pianist popular in Manhattan musical circles.

After *Warming Up*, Paramount considered casting Arthur opposite rising star Gary Cooper in *Legion of the Condemned*, a major studio picture in 1928. But the part eventually went to fellow contractee Fay Wray, and Paramount loaned their new ingénue to MGM instead for *Brotherly Love*. This was a prison satire casting her opposite Karl Dane and George K. Arthur. She was the warden's daughter and the object of both co-stars' affections—until a climactic football game results in an Arthur-to-Arthur fadeout. Like *Warming Up*, *Brotherly Love* featured sound effects and a musical score, but also some scenes with spoken dialogue. Apparently, those scenes didn't involve Jean Arthur, for she was among a clutch of Paramount contract players wary of whether the inevitable switch to talkies might spell the end of her film career. In any case, all contractees were to be tested for sound, with the result that Hollywood speech coaches were suddenly much in demand for private consultations.

JA and Karl Dane in Brotherly Love
(Metro-Goldwyn-Mayer Pictures, 1928).

Although those who failed were few, Jean Arthur was sure she'd be unacceptable for talking pictures, especially after recoiling from her test with the self-judgment "a foghorn!" Years later, Paramount chief executive Adolph Zukor recalled Arthur's reaction to the microphone in his autobiography: "It was that foghorn quality which made her a greater star than she might have become on the silent screen."

Actually, that unique Jean Arthur voice that moviegoers took to in the 1930s and '40s, with its throaty "breaks" and occasional childish tones, would take some years to establish itself.

She returned to her home studio for a supporting part in *Sins of the Fathers*, a vehicle for Paramount's German star, the renowned character actor Emil Jannings. Broadway import Ruth Chatterton had the picture's female lead, while fourth-billed Arthur played his adult daughter, a role overlooked by the film's critics. Like both of her prior 1928 efforts, *Sins of the Fathers* was essentially a silent picture featuring a musical score and sound effects.

Shot in the fall of 1928, *The Canary Murder Case* would have been Jean Arthur's last silent film. In fact, so rapidly was the industry converting to sound that Paramount decided to release it as a talkie. Director Frank Tuttle was thus engaged to redo much of the footage completed by Malcolm St. Clair.

*The Canary Murder Case* is best remembered today as the picture that ruined the Hollywood career of iconic flapper Louise Brooks. Having completed her scenes and gone to Germany to star in *Pandora's Box* for director G. W. Pabst, she was partying in New York when Paramount summoned her back to re-shoot *The Canary Murder Case*. When she refused the studio's demands, they were forced to hire another actress, with the result that Margaret Livingston dubbed her voice in some scenes and doubled for her in others. The results were neither satisfactory nor convincing, and Paramount saw to it that Brooks' future roles in American movies were quite insignificant.

On a more positive note, *The Canary Murder Case* afforded its male star, William Powell, his first assignment as Philo Vance, the popular literary detective of novelist S. S. Van Dine (the pseudonym of Willard Huntington Wright), who was given credit for the book's screen adaptation. Concerned with the killing of a blackmailing nightclub entertainer (Brooks), the movie offered Arthur a subsidiary role as the love interest for third-billed James Hall. In her talkie debut, she failed to make any distinct impression. Her diction is clear, but her delivery stiff. Looking back on what Jean Arthur had to offer in 1929, she analyzed her talents:

"I was a very poor actress in those days. You know—blah! I was awfully anxious to improve, but I was inexperienced so far as genuine training was concerned; I was horribly meek and not of sufficient consequence to be bothered with. Only if you're a great hit do they give you the attention you need. If you've learned some acting technique on the stage, you have a background of references. I presumed there was only one way to enact every emotion, and so I plugged along pretty blindly."

Just before the early-1929 release of *The Canary Murder Case*, Arthur was selected by the Western Association of Motion Picture Advertisers to be among their latest crop of "Wampus Baby Stars." From 1922 to 1934, these executives would select and publicize just such a group of promising young starlets, and in 1929 their ranks also included Sally Blane, Betty Boyd, Ethlyne Clair, Doris Dawson, Josephine Dunn, Helen Foster, Doris Hill, Caryl Lincoln, Anita Page, Mona Rico, Helen Twelvetrees and Loretta Young.

Phillips Holmes and JA in Stairs of Sand (Paramount Pictures, 1929).

Instead of exploiting their new Wampus Baby Star's potential, Paramount assigned her to *Stairs of Sand*, a routine Zane Grey Western, quickly produced to complete the studio contract of a rude, rambunctious Wallace Beery. For Arthur, the movie's only saving grace was her leading man, Phillips Holmes, on whom she developed a crush. It was an attraction the 20-year-old actor failed to reciprocate.

Arthur's disillusionment over the mediocre path of her career at Paramount was then at such a low ebb that, as she later described it, she cornered a studio executive in his office, burst into tears and confessed: "I can't do it. I'm rotten. I'm no good. I can't go on."

Apparently that encounter resulted in an encouraging pep talk and a leading role in a more interesting film, *The Mysterious Dr. Fu Manchu*, based on a melodramatic Sax Rohmer novel. Perhaps encouraged by that Paramount executive's confidence, Arthur brought a more natural, relaxed quality to her portrayal of the diabolical doctor's adopted daughter. In what would now be considered an offensively racist picture, she's hypnotized into helping her father carry out his evil plans against those he holds responsible for the deaths of his wife and son, until she's rescued by fiancé Neil Hamilton. In a typical Hollywood casting ploy, Scandinavian Warner Oland played Fu Manchu; perhaps it was thought that a Swedish accent was equally acceptable to an Asian one. Produced with some care to sets, costumes and lighting, *The Mysterious Dr. Fu Manchu* not only won critical approval, but also kind words for its female star. Perhaps she enjoyed an unusual rapport with her director, for Rowland V. Lee later explained: "Jean Arthur was a lovely looking girl, but had a low, rather husky voice. So, with the advent of sound, no one on the lot would cast her. I thought the quality of her voice would be an added attraction and give color to her performance—which it did."

Arthur's fourth of six 1929 releases was another Philo Vance mystery *The Greene Murder Case*, again featuring William Powell in a follow-up to the successful *Canary Murder Case*. This one, however, was shot as a talkie, although, like many of that year's pictures, it was released in both sound and silent versions, because many of America's cinemas were as yet unequipped for sound. In a role coincidentally employing her own real surname, Arthur plays the ingenuous adopted daughter of a well-to-do family whose members are being methodically killed off by Arthur, who had inherited her birth-father's insanity.

In a 1939 interview with *Screenland's* Maud Cheatham, Arthur recalled this early period in her career:

"I bumped into every kind of disappointment, and was frustrated at every turn. Roles promised me were given to other players, pictures that offered me a chance were shelved, no one was particularly interested in me, and I had not developed a strength of personality to make anyone believe I had special talents. I wanted so desperately to succeed that I drove myself relentlessly, taking no time off for pleasures, or for friendships—yet aiming at the stars. I was still floundering."

A typical starlet fashion pose (Paramount Pictures, 1929).

By now, David Selznick was unofficially engaged to Irene Mayer, a move that would be politically expedient to his future as an important producer. His continued interest in Jean Arthur moved him to secure her the second female lead in a Clara Bow vehicle, *The Saturday Night Kid*. This was a talkie remake of Paramount's 1926 silent *Love 'Em and Leave 'Em*, with Arthur in the role originally played by Louise Brooks, that of Bow's whiny, opportunistic younger sister who's not above stealing her sibling's money and beau (James Hall). Cast in bit parts were future sex symbol Jean Harlow and an attractive young man named Frank Ross.

Clara Bow, Jean Harlow and JA in The Saturday Night Kid
(Paramount Pictures, 1929).

In the critical consensus, many considered Arthur the best thing about *The Saturday Night Kid,* judging her performance more believable than the heavy dramatics displayed by Clara Bow. Many years later, interviewed by Bow biographer David Stenn, Arthur spoke glowingly of the film's more famous star: "She was so generous, no snootiness or anything. She was wonderful to me."

*Half Way to Heaven*, the last of Arthur's six 1929 releases, paired her romantically with the popular Charles "Buddy" Rogers as tightrope walkers whose future together is seriously threatened by the jealousy of colleague Paul Lukas. A less important studio picture than *The Saturday Night Kid*, this one garnered favorable notices for Arthur, including *Variety*'s critic, who observed that she had "a soft, husky voice, which isn't hard to take."

With canine pal (Paramount Pictures, circa 1929).

In a February, 1930 *Photoplay* article headlined "Did She Steal Clara's Picture?" writer Margaret Stuart paints an odd, unorthodox portrait of Arthur, whose own words describe "a negative personality" of little interest to the moviegoing public:

> "All great actresses have had colorful lives. I've never done anything . . . I myself have never been anything, that's why I like to act now. I like to be somebody else."

17

David Selznick's influence then secured her a role in *Street of Chance*, a William Powell vehicle loosely based on the story of notorious Manhattan gambler Arnold Rothstein. Directed by John Cromwell, the picture was among Paramount's more prestigious 1930 offerings, with Arthur billed fourth after Powell, Kay Francis and Regis Toomey, whose wife she played, but to little effect. In fact, Cromwell foresaw no future for her in the movies, and even advised her to return East.

Instead, she returned to leading roles in *Young Eagles*, once again opposite Charles "Buddy" Rogers, as an American spy passing as a German spy in an aviation melodrama directed by William Wellman. Although serving to reunite the star and director of 1927's blockbuster *Wings, Young Eagles* was hardly comparable. It did nothing for Jean Arthur's career, but the movie once again cast her with supporting player Frank Ross, with whom she realized a mutual attraction.

Four years her junior, the Boston-born Ross was a Princeton graduate who had worked in construction and real estate in New York, where he'd had some success in society circles as an amateur singer. When his musical talent drew the attention of Paramount, Ross was signed to a short-term movie contract in 1929, prompting him and his brother Richard to relocate their business to Los Angeles. Although accounts of their meeting with Arthur would vary, it seems that the Ross brothers lived on the same Hollywood street as the Greene family, and got to know "this cute girl" they had noticed in the neighborhood. Indeed, Arthur may have helped Frank Ross get his roles in *The Saturday Night Kid* and *Young Eagles*, but that appears to have been the extent of his screen career, despite the original interest in him as a singer. Determining

JA poses for a 1930
Paramount portrait.

that a Hollywood acting career was not in the cards for him, Ross returned to New York to concentrate on the building business. He and Arthur would remain in close touch through letters and the telephone.

Oddly enough, the producers of the all-star revue *Paramount on Parade* had no use for Frank Ross, while assigning the musically untalented Jean Arthur to one song number and a hospital skit pairing her with comic Leon Errol.

Along with Richard Arlen, Virginia Bruce, Mary Brian, Gary Cooper, James Hall, Phillips Holmes, David Newell, Joan Peers and Fay Wray, she performed in "Let Us Drink to the Girl of My Dreams," one of several segments of the film photographed in the early two-strip Technicolor process.

It was closely followed by her third release in the spring of 1930, *The Return of Dr. Fu Manchu,* whose title says it all. If this melodrama, reuniting her with Warner Oland and Neil Hamilton, seemed a cut above its forerunner, that might be attributable to the ongoing improvements in sound technique.

In search of anything that might improve her opportunities, Arthur sought to alter her pretty but plain starlet image by changing her hair color from brown to a subtle shade of blonde. As she would reflect back on it:

> "Mary Brian was the ace ingénue on the lot and somehow it was said that we looked like each other. That was hard on me, for Mary was so much better than I was, and so much bigger box office, that she was inevitably first choice. I got the ultra insipid assignments. It dawned on me that if I lightened my hair a little, it would lessen any resemblance. So far as the studio was concerned, I dyed in vain."

Joel McCrea and JA in The Silver Horde (RKO Radio Pictures, 1930).

With little else to offer their unhappy starlet, Paramount then loaned her out to RKO for a pair of routine melodramas, *Danger Lights* and *The Silver*

*Horde*, both released in the latter half of 1930. Neither gave Arthur any role challenges. In the former, she was romanced by both Robert Armstrong and Louis Wolheim when they weren't otherwise engaged in more exciting railroad action. *The Silver Horde* offered Arthur the thankless part of a holier-than-thou society girl who understandably loses Joel McCrea to the film's more colorful "bad girl" Evelyn Brent.

Back at Paramount, she appeared opposite Jack Oakie in the mobster parody *The Gang Buster*, in which she was kidnapped by crooks and eventually rescued by Oakie. A. Edward Sutherland directed this entertaining "B" picture, and *Variety* found numerous elements deserving of praise, singling out Jean Arthur in her most substantial part since *The Saturday Night Kid*.

Jack Oakie and JA in The Gang Buster (Paramount Pictures, 1931).

Arthur long thought about acting on the stage, and already had several offers when she embraced one such opportunity and appeared in the Pasadena Playhouse production of Bella Spewack's drama *Spring Song*, which played for a 10-day run in December, 1930. In a preview of her theatrical future, she suffered an attack of opening-night nerves, informing director Gilmore Brown that she couldn't go on. But words of encouragement apparently solved the problem, and enabled Jean Arthur to enjoy her first encounter with an exciting new experience—the enthusiastic applause of a live audience.

JA sits for the Universal portrait photographer (1931).

Having made a local success onstage, she hoped that might lead to better parts. Instead, she was loaned out to Universal for the slight comedy *The Virtuous Husband* opposite Elliott Nugent, and *Ex-Bad Boy*, reuniting her with Robert Armstrong. Rounding out her Paramount contract was the multi-star crime drama *The Lawyer's Secret*, in which she had fifth billing as Richard Arlen's fiancée, but perhaps the movie's best role as the one who tracks down the killer. Despite its cast, *The Lawyer's Secret* didn't excite the critics. The *New York Times* expressed pleasure in watching Jean Arthur and Fay Wray, but apparently Paramount was less impressed: for in the spring of 1931, the studio failed to renew the contracts of either star, as well as Mary Brian. With the Paramount careers of Clara Bow and Nancy Carroll also on the wane, there was stronger interest in the fresh, new personalities of Marlene Dietrich, Carole Lombard, Sylvia Sidney, Claudette Colbert and Tallulah Bankhead.

Fay Wray, Clive Brook and JA in *The Lawyer's Secret*
(Paramount Pictures, 1931).

Reflecting on that turning point, Arthur told writer Ben Maddox for a 1935 *Motion Picture* article:

"I had been in Hollywood long enough to know which way the wind was blowing. If I couldn't get stronger parts with the studio where I'd been, why expect the others to have faith in me? I knew I had potentialities, but no one else sensed it. So I just quit altogether! I realized I wasn't demonstrating any noble ability. I didn't comprehend what was wrong with me, but I was sure of two things by then: something was, and no one intended to show me how to advance.

"Playing those colorless, vapid ingénues had bored me so I just couldn't go on. I didn't want to. I'd saved money, so I didn't have to. What's more, along had come 'the man.' He lived in New York and I simply abandoned all future dreams of a career. If it wasn't to be first class, I didn't want it. The salary I could have earned by hanging on and taking whatever I could get in the same sickly sweet rut wasn't enough lure."

Jean Arthur returned to Manhattan in the autumn of 1931 amid the Great Depression. Centered on Long Island, Frank Ross was comfortable enough to concentrate on the acquisition of reasonably-priced land for future development. Arthur had saved enough of her Hollywood money to support herself for the present, while entertaining old ideas of teaching or interior design, careers not then very lucrative. Acting in the theatre, however, was a likely alternative, and her eight years of Hollywood experience sufficiently impressed agent Chamberlain Brown to get her a role in Gilbert Seldes' adaptation of the classic Greek comedy *Lysistrata*, which opened at New York City's uptown Riviera Theatre on 96th Street in January of 1932 and toured until March, when it closed at Mount Vernon's Westchester County Center. In a large cast featuring Thais Lawton and Sydney Greenstreet, her role of Kalonika paid her the then-impressive theatrical wage of $50 a week.

Shortly after *Lysistrata*'s closing, Arthur was cast in her first Broadway play, the Paul Hervey Fox–George Tilton comedy *Foreign Affairs*. This was a production of the distinguished Theatre Guild that starred Henry Hull, Dorothy Gish and Osgood Perkins, and cast Arthur in the supporting role of a kitchen maid romantically involved with sophisticated diplomat Hull at a provincial Italian inn. Once again, nerves challenged Arthur's opening-night ability to perform ("When I walked on, I wasn't sure any noise would emerge from my lips"). But she did well enough to please the newspaper reviewers: the *New York Times* included her among cast members performing "with considerable skill"; the *New York Sun* dubbed her "dryly witty"; and the *World-Telegram* called her "a vivid Anna," adding "she and Mr. Perkins easily outshine the others." It opened on April 13, 1932 at the Avon Theatre, but failed to sufficiently impress critics or attract the public, closing after 23 performances.

Best of all, *Foreign Affairs* gave Jean Arthur the opportunity to work alongside seasoned stage professionals in the nightly repetition of performance before a live audience, a learning experience not available in Hollywood moviemaking.

Frank Ross (Paramount Pictures, 1929).

On June 11, 1932, a month after the last performance of *Foreign Affairs*, Jean Arthur very quietly married Frank K. Ross Jr. at the Church-in-the-Gardens in Forest Hills, Queens. The nuptials were carried out in such secrecy that it wasn't until four months later that even a *rumor* reached the Los Angeles press. In fact, not even her Hollywood-based father appeared to know of the union. Among the personal traits they shared, Arthur and Ross treasured their privacy.

In lieu of a honeymoon, Jean Arthur immediately departed for Philadelphia and the female lead, opposite Claude Rains, in the Jean Bart melodrama *The Man Who Reclaimed His Head.* Opening on June 16th, this tryout was successful enough to insure its Broadway production the following September. During the play's summer hiatus, before the resumption of pre-Broadway rehearsals, Arthur took on a summer-stock engagement with the Monmouth County Players, a new group set up to perform an eight-week season of theatrical revivals in Red Bank, New Jersey. She would appear in the first three plays: Robert E. Sherwood's *The Road to Rome*, Rachel Crothers' *Let Us Be Gay*, and the more serious *Coquette* by George Abbott and Ann Preston Bridges. The experience of weekly stock in the company of such veterans as Alice Brady, Jean Adair, McKay Morris and Jessie Ralph could only have proved invaluable to Arthur, especially when removed from the critical eyes of Broadway reviewers.

With only three weeks to relax and enjoy life as Mrs. Frank Ross, Jean Arthur was back rehearsing for *The Man Who Reclaimed his Head*, under the direction of Herbert J. Biberman. On September 8th, the play opened at the Broadhurst Theatre in a spectacular, large-cast production that proved more impressive than its script. For Arthur, there was the valuable experience of working with Rains ("He taught me a lot"). There was also the negative criticism of Brooks Atkinson: "Her voice needs considerable cultivation." The play endured for 28 performances.

An offer from RKO of a role in *The Past of Mary Holmes* coincided with a visit to her parents in California that Thanksgiving, when Arthur made her first motion picture in two years. Billed third, after Helen MacKellar (in the title role) and Eric Linden, she only seems to have taken this routine romantic part because the studio paid for her round-trip train fare, plus expenses. The *New York Times* noted some improvement in her acting.

Back in New York, Arthur had a leading role in the most mysterious of all her 1930s films, a local production called *Get That Venus*, directed by Grover Lee for Regent Pictures. The independent movie starred Ernest Truex and featured a cast of Manhattan actors in a muddled plot concerning the theft of a Venus painting. Because the film was not copyrighted or apparently released in the U.S., with no reviews ever appearing in any of the usual publications, *Get That Venus* appears lost to obscurity. But since this writer was present at a private 8mm screening in the 1960s, the movie is known to exist, although its details are but a dim memory. That it made so little impression at the time may explain a lot.

Tom Howard, Harry Davenport, JA and Ernest Truex in Get That Venus (Regent Pictures, 1933).

The Broadway stage continued to find a place for Jean Arthur, and on May 10, 1933 she opened at the Masque Theatre in a play by Gladys Unger and Leyla Georgie called *$25 an Hour*. The actor Thomas Mitchell directed a cast that included Georges Metaxa and Olga Baclanova, drawing the *New York Times* approval of Mitchell's direction and Arthur's performance, but little else. The *Herald Tribune*'s critic also liked her work, opining "Twice this season I have seen her in stage dramas of no importance, and each time she has shown herself as an interesting and attractive actress." The play closed after 22 performances.

If her plays failed to make an impression, at least her acting did, with Hollywood executives visiting Arthur backstage and expressing interest in her services. In a later interview, she recalled responding: "Thank you very much, but I'm staying here on Broadway. You see, they let me act."

With the demise of *$25 an Hour*, Arthur and her husband finally managed a delayed, month-long honeymoon when friends offered them the use of an Adirondacks lodge.

And then it was another theatrical engagement for Arthur, performing as the daughter of character actress Esther Dale, in a summer-stock tryout of the comedy *Perhaps We Are* with the Hampton Players of Southampton, New York. Again, there was considerable praise for the Hollywood fugitive's talent, helping to build the confidence she had always lacked in motion pictures. Observers noted her more relaxed acting style and her penchant for light comedy. And with her increased activity in the living theatre, the nerves and shyness that had once inhibited her work appeared no longer a problem:

> "I learned to face audiences and forget them. To see the footlights and not to see them; to gauge the reactions of hundreds of people, and yet to throw myself so completely into a role that I was oblivious to their reaction."

From her short engagement in *Perhaps We Are*, the actress went directly into rehearsals for another Broadway play, *The Curtain Rises* by Benjamin M. Kaye (writing under the exotic pen name Oskar Rempel). This was a romantic comedy in which Arthur's character evolves from frumpish spinster to accomplished actress. The reviewers liked her work as well as that of her leading man, Donald Foster. Brooks Atkinson called them "the only forthright actors in the cast." Their director was her *Get That Venus* colleague, Ernest Truex, and although the play itself received mixed notices, it was not only Jean Arthur's most successful Broadway show of this period, but also her favorite. It ran from October to December of 1933, racking up 61 performances—a run that might have been extended except for her rather bizarre behavior. *Variety* even reported on the star's "temperament," commenting on her refusal to pose for cast photos and an unpopular insistence on open doors backstage, despite the cold weather.

When she paid a Christmas visit to her family in California, she received a number of offers to sign movie contracts, which she characteristically rejected. But a one-picture deal with little, upcoming Columbia Pictures intrigued her, and she agreed to appear opposite Jack Holt in *Whirlpool* (1934), because it was a good dramatic part. Today, one can note her portrayal of this brash newspaper reporter as both more interesting than most of her prior movie performances, and also the earliest example of the sort of forthright screen character she'd best be known for.

Jack Holt and JA in Whirlpool (Columbia Pictures, 1934).

In a screenplay that could easily have drifted overboard in its sentimentality, *Whirlpool* won plaudits for the now-very-blonde Jean Arthur for keeping things under control. In the New York *Herald Tribune*, Howard Barnes thought veteran star Holt out-acted by her "brilliant and thoroughly plausible portrayal of a difficult role, marking her as a first-rate actress."

Prior to this movie's completion, Columbia was impressed with Arthur's footage, which reflected a screen image much changed from her Paramount days. Her confident manner and stage-educated way with dialogue now revealed what her earlier screen work had been lacking, and the studio offered her a five-year contract.

Arthur considered her two-year Broadway sojourn "the happiest years of my life." They had enabled her to learn from masters of the theatre. She was happy living in New York with her husband, and enjoying the excitement that actors can only experience performing before live audiences. And yet, the often-brief runs of her plays had meant frequent bouts of unemployment during a difficult economic time. Signing the average movie contract would mean being away from her husband, as well as Broadway. But it also offered proximity to the Greene clan, and certainly a handsome and steady income. Before signing that contract, Arthur instituted a clause that would permit her return to New York for stage work once a year. For its part, Columbia could engage her services for up to four movies a year.

Under her new contract, Jean Arthur went on to act in two more 1934 pictures for the studio before returning to Broadway. *The Defense Rests* cast her again opposite Jack Holt, who had portrayed her racketeer-father in *Whirlpool*. This time, Holt was an unethical lawyer challenged by Arthur's character, a recent law-school graduate who eventually falls for her older opponent. *The Defense Rests* offered standard melodramatics, perhaps a cut below *Whirlpool*, and *Variety*'s critic found neither star credible as lawyers.

*The Most Precious Thing in Life* offered Arthur the challenge of progressing from youth to old age in a tear-jerking story of mother love and sacrifice. The actress had eagerly approached the idea of playing beyond her years, but although wigged and made up to look older, she wasn't convincing, physically. As *Variety* commented, she looked like nothing more than "a young woman in elderly makeup." On the plus side, despite taking second billing to Richard Cromwell, who played her son, Arthur was for the first time a film's main focus.

Richard Cromwell and JA in The Most Precious Thing in Life
(Columbia Pictures, 1934).

In the spring of 1934, she was back in New York to begin rehearsals for another stage play, Ruth Langner's adaptation of Otto Indig's Hungarian comedy *The Bride of Torozko*. In it, she played a peasant girl whose Catholic wedding plans are called off when it's revealed that she's really Jewish. Van Heflin portrayed the discouraged fiancé and Sam Jaffe the Hebrew tavern keeper who takes her under his wing. Eventually, it turns out that she's actually a Protestant. In the *New York Times*, Brooks Atkinson found her "modestly enchanting," while John Mason Brown, writing in the *Post*, thought her talents wasted in an unworthy vehicle, but concluded, "Miss Arthur is a young actress who matches her sincerity and her skill with her charm and beauty."

As Klari in the 1934 Broadway production of The Bride of Torozko
(author's collection).

She expressed a desire to experience a long run in a stage play, but *The Bride of Torozko* was not to be the one. It had begun summer tryouts on July 9th in Westport, Connecticut, and opened September 13th on Broadway at Henry Miller's Theatre, lasting for a brief 12 performances.

In the short course of less than three years, Jean Arthur had performed in no less than 10 stage productions, from which she gained a tremendous amount of knowledge, experience and self-assurance. It would be 11 years before she'd again return to the theatre, because her next movie would offer the actress that long-awaited break-through role.

JA, Louella Parsons and Edward G. Robinson at a CBS radio broadcast
of Hollywood Hotel on February 1, 1935.

*The Whole Town's Talking* was an inspired collaboration between Robert Riskin and Jo Swerling, adapting a story by W. R. Burnett about a mild-mannered clerk who's the look-alike of a gangster wanted for murder. That resemblance eventually enables the clerk to help police track down the killer, and he emerges an unexpected hero. On loan from heavier assignments at Warner Bros., Edward G. Robinson displays wonderful versatility in this dual role, with Arthur cast as his supportive co-worker, a self-possessed stenographer.

John Ford, who had directed the actress in *Cameo Kirby*, her first feature film 11 years earlier, guided this offbeat blend of humor and melodrama. In support of Robinson, Arthur has much less time onscreen, and yet she makes a major impression in a part that might have seemed ordinary with a lesser actress. The picture was released at the end of February 1935, and its press reception was enthusiastic. In his 1973 autobiography *All My Yesterdays*, Robinson acknowledged his own critical approval before shifting to their raves about Jean Arthur—"that curious, neurotic actress with so touching and appealing a nature that she really brought a new dimension to the screen." With reference to her "voice that grated like fresh peppermint," he went on to recall: "She was whimsical without being silly; unique without being nutty, a theatrical personality who was an untheatrical person. She was a delight to work with and to know."

To *Variety*'s critic, Arthur was a revelation: "She's gone blonde and fresh. Effect on her personality is to produce a new girl. But a better type. She's more individualistic, more typically the young American self-reliant, rather sassy stenog."

JA and Edward G. Robinson in The Whole Town's Talking
(Columbia Pictures, 1935).

Other opportunities would now come her way, and they would inevitably reflect that unique quality she initially revealed so charmingly in *The Whole Town's Talking*. For the next decade, Jean Arthur would be most closely identified with the goodhearted working girl whose irreverent enthusiasm inspires a less forceful male to realize his potential.

Before *Town's* release, she completed another, less important Columbia picture, the comedy-drama *Party Wire*, about small-town rumors spread by telephone gossip. Its only claim to importance: for the first time on screen, Jean Arthur was given top billing.

She was then loaned out to MGM for *Public Hero #1* and Universal for *Diamond Jim*, before returning to her home studio for *The Public Menace* and *If You Could Only Cook*. All told, there were six Jean Arthur pictures released in 1935. This proliferation of her onscreen image would not be repeated during any future calendar year.

*Public Hero #1* is an odd but entertaining mixture of fast-moving melodrama and occasional light comedy, with Chester Morris as a G-Man who goes undercover to gain the confidence of gangsters and bring them to justice. In a wisecracking role reminiscent of her character in *The Whole Town's Talking*, Arthur's the sister of crime boss Joseph Calleia, nevertheless finding a measure of romance with the ungallant G-Man. Billed second, after supporting actor Lionel Barrymore, she ranked high with the movie's critics.

Chester Morris, Lionel Barrymore and JA in Public Hero #1
(Metro-Goldwyn-Mayer, 1935).

*Diamond Jim*, loosely based on a biography of Diamond Jim Brady, was mostly a vehicle for character actor Edward Arnold, concentrating on the females in his life. In a dual role as two of those women, Jean Arthur plays first a Southern belle, then a calculating gold-digger who ends up with another man (Cesar Romero). Probably because of her recognizably unusual voice, Arthur was awkwardly dubbed by another actress for the first, and briefer, characterization. Under the circumstances, director A. Edward Sutherland (*The Saturday Night Kid, The Gang Buster*) did the best he could.

Back at Columbia, she was successfully teamed with George Murphy in the gangster comedy *The Public Menace*, a minor but entertaining programmer well directed by Erle C. Kenton (*The Island of Lost Souls*).

Gangsters also figure in the plot of *If You Could Only Cook*, about an unemployed young woman (Arthur), who meets an auto manufacturer (Herbert Marshall) on a park bench. Posing as a married couple, they find employment in the household of crooks. The storyline suggests more potential then is realized by either the script or director William A. Seiter. The movie was Columbia's 1935 Christmas release, and Jean Arthur's performance once more drew critical approbation.

Herbert Marshall and JA in If You Could Only Cook
(Columbia Pictures 1935).

By now, the actress had sufficiently proven her value to Columbia Pictures that the studio's crass, famously difficult chief honcho Harry Cohn conceded her such rare, contractual privileges as script and director approval. Nevertheless, her next big break would come almost by accident.

Having brought minor-league Columbia unexpected prestige and widespread industry respect with his Oscar-sweeping romantic comedy *It Happened One Night*, contract director Frank Capra was preparing to film a Clarence Budington Kelland story called "Opera Hat," starring Gary Cooper as a small-town Vermonter who inherits a fortune, and learns to deal with big-city corruption. For the female lead, a cynical newspaperwoman, former Capra heroines Barbara Stanwyck and Loretta Young were considered before the studio signed Carole Lombard. But Lombard opted out three days before the start of production to do *My Man Godfrey* instead. A week into filming, Capra finally cast Columbia contractee Arthur, against the advice of Harry Cohn, who carped about her odd voice. Cohn also pointed out that, while her face looked attractively feminine on the left side, it took on a masculine aspect on the right. Having dealt with a similar problem directing Claudette Colbert in *It Happened One Night*, Capra knew how to handle the situation, in league with cameraman Joseph Walker. This would be a valuable "learning" experience for Jean Arthur, discovering the importance of how she should be photographed.

JA, Gary Cooper and Ruth Donnelly in Mr. Deeds Goes to Town
(Columbia Pictures, 1936).

Released in mid-April of 1936 as *Mr. Deeds Goes to Town*, this time-honored comedy finally established the actress as a major movie star. Capra, who later directed Arthur in two other 1930s classics, *You Can't Take It With You* and *Mr. Smith Goes to Washington*, termed her his favorite actress. Of her performance in *Mr. Deeds Goes to Town*, he would say: "Some actresses could have played the cynical part, while others could have done the romantic ending. But no one could have done them both as well as Jean."

At Columbia during this prolific period of her best work, colleagues mostly remembered Arthur for her professionalism, as well as her shyness. Despite her success, she "was never sure of herself," remembered Columbia character player Ann Doran, who appeared in several films with her. Arthur was also known for not mixing with fellow cast or crew members during production, as well as providing headaches for the wardrobe department. In the opinion of *Deeds* cinematographer Joseph Walker, "There was nothing wrong with her except insecurity."

*Mr. Deeds Goes to Town*, although reasonably well received by the press, did not initially receive the raves one might have expected, considering its now—classic status. However, at year's end it was named Best Picture by the New York Film Critics, as well as the National Board of Review. And at the 1937 Academy Awards ceremony, the movie brought Frank Capra his second Best Director Oscar.

The late-Depression year 1936 saw Jean Arthur making the impressive salary of $119,000, enabling her to finance a better life for her parents, including bigger and more comfortable housing. She also made possible her brother Don's dream of owning a restaurant, and arranged for sibling Bob to become a studio grip.

With her increased visibility in important movies, Arthur now found it more difficult to maintain her valued privacy. Fan magazines and newspapers pursued her for stories and interviews, and were frequently frustrated by her elusiveness. On occasions when he was visiting, Frank Ross helped fend off intrusive questions. Arthur was also forced to deal with queries about their unusual bicoastal relationship:

> "It was during this separation from my husband that I rediscovered that no career could satisfy me. I wanted to live my emotions, and I realized that a woman's highest goal is marriage and a home. Before long, Frank and I agreed that our happiness lay out here, and together. We wanted no more separations."

JA and William Powell in The Ex Mrs. Bradford
(RKO Radio Pictures, 1936).

The security of Arthur's mid-1930s Hollywood stardom finally moved New York-based Frank Ross to end the need for intermittent husband-and-wife visitations. Arthur preferred the East Coast, but realized her current livelihood was in Hollywood, motivating Ross to close his Long Island operations and relocate to L.A. There, he managed to land a job as production assistant at the studios of filmmaker Hal Roach.

Having for some time shared her parents' home, Arthur now reunited with Ross in renting both a Beverly Hills mansion and a Malibu beach house, where director Capra and screenwriter Jo Swerling were among her neighbors.

Although she resented the money Harry Cohn would make from loaning her out to other studios, she enjoyed working once more with her old Philo Vance teammate William Powell in RKO's *The Ex-Mrs. Bradford*. The comparisons to Powell's earlier hit *The Thin Man* were inescapable with this "screwball" comedy-mystery about a racetrack murder that involves a divorced couple turned amateur sleuths. In his complimentary *New York Times* review, Frank Nugent made reference to *The Thin Man*'s leading lady, Myrna Loy:

> "This time it is Jean Arthur instead of Miss Loy who assists Mr. Powell, and disclaiming the cries of 'treason' from the loyal Loyites, we must proclaim our complete satisfaction with the change. Miss Arthur is an amusing little clown who manages to be Mr. Powell's best friend and severest handicap without ever quite convincing us that she is just a nitwit."

William Powell and JA in The Ex-Mrs. Bradford
(RKO Radio Pictures, 1936).

*The Ex-Mrs. Bradford* was quickly but slickly made, with Arthur never looking more attractive than in the uncharacteristically glamorous wardrobe created for her by Bernard Newman, the designer responsible for Ginger Rogers' sophisticated look in many of her RKO teamings with Fred Astaire.

After making three pictures in succession, Arthur was ready for a break to enjoy time off with her husband. But any such consideration was lost upon Harry Cohn, who immediately assigned her to an additional pair of Columbia films, *Adventure in Manhattan* and *More Than a Secretary*.

*Adventure in Manhattan* reunited the actress with Joel McCrea, her earlier colleague from *The Silver Horde*, a movie in which she'd lost him to nominal star Evelyn Brent. This time they'd enjoy the fadeout together, although their vehicle was a convoluted blend of mystery and comedy with McCrea as a criminologist and Arthur as a stage actress who become romantically involved in a farfetched tale of jewel thievery. The none-too-credible script drew criticism from the reviewers, who nevertheless liked both stars' performances.

JA, Joel McCrea and Reginald Owen in Adventure in Manhattan
(Columbia Pictures, 1936).

*More Than a Secretary*, her fourth and final 1936 release, teamed Arthur with George Brent, under the direction of veteran Alfred E. Green, in a pleasant but trivial romantic farce set in the world of magazine publishing. Considering the story weaknesses of her most recent movies for Columbia, one wonders whether Arthur was actually exercising her contractual right to script approval.

JA and George Brent in More Than a Secretary
(Columbia Pictures, 1936).

Whatever dissatisfaction she may then have had with her Columbia assignments was alleviated by a subsequent loan-out to Paramount for producer-director Cecil B. DeMille's expensive, large-scale Western epic *The Plainsman*. No matter that Arthur still hadn't had that long-desired vacation, here was the chance to portray Calamity Jane, a truly emancipated woman whose historical existence amid the 19th-century Western plains was both legendary and notorious.

Based on books about the famed Wild Bill Hickok (to be played by a well-cast Gary Cooper), the fanciful screenplay by the triumvirate of Waldemar Young, Harold Lamb and Lynn Riggs played fast and loose with documented history to weave a romantic, typically DeMille fiction that pretended to portray a number of celebrated historical figures with careless disregard for fact.

JA and Gary Cooper in The Plainsman (Paramount Pictures, 1937).

In his autobiography, the filmmaker allows as how he took "some liberties with authenticity" by casting Jean Arthur as the coarse, amoral and mannishly unattractive brunette Calamity (aka Martha Jane Canary). But this was only after he'd tried unsuccessfully to engage Mae West!

Fired up to attempt an authentic portrayal, Arthur expressed plans to go without makeup, crop her hair short and approximate the real Calamity Jane as closely as possible. DeMille would have no part of such a concept, with the result that *The Plainsman*'s leading lady is artfully made-up, beautifully blonde-coiffed and merely engagingly tomboyish. Historians may have blanched at her characterization, but audiences loved it. And she got to crack a mean bullwhip.

All told, *The Plainsman* was a cunningly contrived audience-pleaser, and among Jean Arthur's personal favorites of her career. The fact that she played opposite her own top-rated leading man, Gary Cooper, may have had something to do with it. She also admired Cooper's professionalism: "He never went up on his lines. He was always there."

Arthur and DeMille apparently harbored a great deal of respect for one another, and although they never worked together again on a movie, she did make numerous appearances on CBS's *Lux Radio Theatre* during the years when he served as its producer and host. Her initial broadcast, shortly following the January 1937 release of *The Plainsman,* was in an hour-long adaptation of *Mr. Deeds Goes to Town*, along with Cooper and supporting player Lionel Stander. Arthur's distinctive sound adapted well to radio, where she quickly learned the techniques of projecting a character through voice alone. Among her subsequent appearances on the *Lux* program would be *Seventh Heaven* (opposite Don Ameche), *Pygmalion* (Brian Aherne), and *Remember the Night* (Fred MacMurray).

Released in January of 1937, *The Plainsman* was the first of three Arthur movies that year, and none of them for her home studio. An additional loan-out was to independent producer Walter Wanger for *History Is Made at Night*, a United Artists release.

The Wanger picture teamed Jean Arthur for the first and only time with suave, Gallic-accented Charles Boyer in a complex stew of farce, romance and melodrama. In retrospect, Arthur would recall *History Is Made at Night* as having been her most sophisticated, elegantly attired role. In the wake of her acclaim for *Mr. Deeds Goes to Town*, it's a curious truth that her best assignments were not then at Columbia. Not only did she resent the fact that Columbia had few roles for her on the home lot, but, worse still, they richly profited from loaning her to other studios, working her nonstop with no extra benefit to her.

As Irene Vail in History Is Made at Night (United Artists, 1937).

In a bid for independence, and despite her contractual obligations to Columbia, Arthur signed with Paramount in the spring of 1937 to star in *Easy Living*. At the same time, she declared that she would henceforth work as a free-lance artist, choosing her future roles without studio interference. Not unexpectedly, Harry Cohn contested her actions, filing an injunction to prevent her from making *Easy Living* and reminding her that she was bound to Columbia for three more years. However, her contract did allow her to film two movies per annum for other studios, and so Cohn failed to cancel her one-picture agreement with Paramount. The worst he could do was institute a court ruling that kept her from accepting stage or radio work for a year.

Like Bette Davis, who went to court against Warner Bros. in 1936 in a fight for better roles, Jean Arthur also made her grievances known: "I wanted to make quality pictures and to amount to something, or else not be in the business."

It's worthy of note that the late-Thirties films of both Davis and Arthur eventually improved, in the wake of their actions.

But first, Jean Arthur returned to Paramount for one of her best comedies, the Preston Sturges screenplay *Easy Living*, inventively directed by Mitchell Leisen. This was a screwball farce that was only moderately successful with critics and audiences in its day, but which has gained minor-classic status with the passage of time, especially for Arthur's performance.

JA gets a last-minute grooming from Director Mitchell Leisen for the Easy Living cameras (Paramount Pictures, 1937).

The film hinges on a case of mistaken identity in which office worker Arthur is thought to be a millionaire's mistress, and finds herself surrounded with luxury. It all begins when a discarded sable coat, flung from a penthouse apartment, falls upon her as she rides atop the Fifth Avenue bus. A memorable highlight is the Automat sequence in which she and romantic lead Ray Milland are caught up in a food fight among the mechanically challenged clientele.

In the wake of *Easy Living*'s completion, Arthur was deeply upset to find her problems with Columbia far from over. Dissatisfied with the pictures that studio had most recently assigned to her, she begged them to acquire rights to George Bernard Shaw's *Pygmalion* for her, but the project was rejected as being old-fashioned. Not that Shaw would likely have agreed, for a British version was already in production starring Wendy Hiller and Leslie Howard. Harry Cohn now planned loaning her out again, this time for a Warner Bros. picture for which she was given no information as to director, cast, subject matter or the film's title. Her understandable refusal immediately put her on suspension, extending her Columbia contract and keeping her from accepting any other Hollywood offers. Not that she wanted to do so. After six movies in a row, she was sorely in need of a rest.

In his 1997 biography of Arthur, John Oller reveals that the actress was sufficiently distressed by Harry Cohn to hatch a "perfect murder" plot to do away with the much-hated Columbia honcho without getting caught. When Frank Ross got wind of her desperate intentions, he intervened and saw to it that they left town for a needed vacation in the picturesque oceanside community of Carmel. For the actress, it was love at first sight, resulting in their taking a lease on the cliffside redwood dwelling called "Driftwood," where she would gradually calm her nerves and generally reclaim her sanity with lengthy beach walks.

Ross was now employed as an aide to independent producer Hal Roach, and had to return to Los Angeles, so Hannah Greene arrived to keep Arthur company at her new home.

By the start of 1938, word was circulating in Hollywood that Jean Arthur had retired from moviemaking for good. Was this a ploy of Harry Cohn's to motivate her return to his studio? Whatever the case, Frank Capra now sought her for his next Columbia assignment, an adaptation of the popular George S. Kaufman-Moss Hart stage farce *You Can't Take It With You*. In a somewhat complicated deal, he got Cohn to purchase Clifford Odets' hit play *Golden Boy,* in which he planned to direct Arthur in the part played on Broadway by Frances Farmer.

With expectations that she would next appear in both of these stage-to-screen projects for Columbia, Arthur terminated her year-long Hollywood exile by signing a new three-year contract with the studio. It would restrict her Columbia obligations to two movies a year, while allowing for one picture elsewhere. She also negotiated a contractual clause freeing her of all publicity duties: she would henceforth not have to make public appearances or grant press interviews in conjunction with her films. This didn't help her already chilly relationship with the Hollywood press.

In *You Can't Take It With You*, Arthur is the "normal" daughter in a family of lovable misfits, whose extended household includes an eccentric collection of oddballs. When her working-class secretary finds romance with boss James Stewart, the firm's vice president, the stage is set for entertaining chaos amidst class snobbery and parental differences.

Robert Riskin, a Capra fixture whose many screenplays had included *It Happened One Night* and *Mr. Deeds Goes to Town*, took considerable liberties in adapting the Kaufman-Hart play to fit the characteristic Capra movie mold. Departing from the play's single living-room set to encompass locales such as a nightclub, jail and office building, he fleshes out the relationship of the Arthur and Stewart characters. And there's a good bit of emphasis on the machinations of Stewart's tycoon father (Edward Arnold) to acquire the residential property of Arthur's disinterested parent (Lionel Barrymore), and replace it with a large factory.

Halliwell Hobbes, Lionel Barrymore, Samuel S. Hinds, Donald Meek, Mischa Auer, JA, Ann Miller and Spring Byington in You Can't Take It With You (Columbia Pictures, 1938).

At 37, Jean Arthur looked remarkably youthful in an era when that would have been considered advanced middle-age, and is totally convincing, even when sliding down a staircase banister. Her subtle changes of character, within the screenplay's structure, endear her to us in a persona necessarily less colorful than most of those around her. However, this was not one of Arthur's favorite roles. She considered it just another straight ingénue, not dissimilar to those that had motivated her departure for the stage a few years earlier.

*You Can't Take It With You* was released in September of 1938 and, despite Arthur's negative feelings, could not have been a better boost to her late-Thirties career. Its popularity with moviegoers was eventually capped with Academy Awards for Best Picture and Best Director Frank Capra. Co-star Stewart would later call Jean Arthur "the finest actress I ever worked with," explaining "No one had her humor, her timing."

Before the completion of the Capra picture, there was talk that Arthur's next would be something called *Water Gypsies*, a Hal Roach project involving Arthur's husband. But Frank Ross was soon named associate producer on Roach's *Of Mice and Men*, and *Water Gypsies* was abandoned.

A far bigger enterprise preoccupied the actress during the second half of 1938, David O. Selznick's much publicized search for Scarlett O'Hara, the willful Dixie heroine of Margaret Mitchell's epic novel, *Gone With the Wind*. Seventy-odd years after British actress Vivien Leigh made the role so vividly her own and took home an Oscar it's difficult to imagine Jean Arthur as Scarlett. However, due partly to her old friendship with Selznick and his steadfast affection for her, she not only tested for the part, but wound up on the producer's final short-list, along with Paulette Goddard, Joan Bennett and Leigh. Ten days prior to the formal announcement of Vivien Leigh, one newspaper even predicted that a reliable source had informed them that Arthur was the finalist. When Selznick made the results known, it's rumored that Jean Arthur burned her print of the screen test.

Despite Frank Capra's earlier notion of starring Jean Arthur in the movie version of *Golden Boy*, he now abandoned that project to fellow director Rouben Mamoulian, in exchange for a script that interested him more. This was the story of an idealistic young man who soon comes to regret his appointment to the U.S. Senate, and its working title was *The Gentleman From Montana*. For his part, Mamoulian's interest in *Golden Boy* did not include Jean Arthur. Instead, he would cast Barbara Stanwyck in the Frances Farmer role. Stanwyck also copped the lead Cecil B. DeMille had originally considered Arthur for in his *Union Pacific*. Arthur's name was also bandied about for several other movies she didn't get to make in that 1939-1940 period: *Good Girls Go to Paris*, eventually starring Joan Blondell, and two pictures that went to Rosalind Russell, *His Girl Friday* and *No Time for Comedy*.

Instead, Arthur would go on to star in two of the most successful films of that celebrated year of 1939: Howard Hawks' *Only Angels Have Wings* and Frank Capra's *Mr. Smith Goes to Washington.*

The Hawks film, produced under its working title of *Pilot No. 4*, teamed Arthur for the first time with Cary Grant in an adventure tale of mail-carrying fliers in South America. Into this predominantly male society, she is oddly cast against type as a stranded showgirl from Brooklyn. Hawks later recalled how Arthur resisted his attempts to turn her into the sort of sexy, self-assured heroine later associated with Lauren Bacall in his mid-Forties dramas *To Have and Have Not* and *The Big Sleep*. Amid filming, Arthur responded, "I can't do that kind of stuff." Despite their on-set differences, Hawks later termed her performance "really good."

*Only Angels Have Wings* brought Jean Arthur other problems with her fellow cast members. What started out as a copasetic relationship with co-star Grant ("he was making jokes all the time") changed considerably when she felt he was rudely upstaging her. And then there was Arthur's attitude toward the film's second female lead, played by the equally shy but undeniably glamorous Rita Hayworth. After a succession of Columbia B-pictures, 21-year-old Hayworth now had a star-making supporting role in a major production. Harry Cohn was more than a little preoccupied with the burgeoning Hayworth career, and Arthur was well aware of its implications. For several years, she had been Columbia's top female, and now there was competition from someone not only more beautiful but also considerably younger.

As Bonnie Lee in Only Angels Have Wings
(Columbia Pictures, 1939).

As Arthur confidante Roddy McDowall later told biographer John Oller, "Jean was very jealous of Rita Hayworth. She thought Rita was put in the film to make her look unattractive, and she hated Harry Cohn over that."

Originally, of course, *Mr. Smith Goes to Washington* was known as *The Gentleman From Montana*. And, for a time, producer/director Capra re-titled it *Mr. Deeds Goes to Washington*, with the idea of re-teaming Jean Arthur and Gary Cooper in a reprise of their earlier collaboration. But contractual obligations bound Cooper to producer Samuel Goldwyn, and so Capra turned back to his most recent male lead, James Stewart.

In retrospect, it's difficult to imagine anyone better cast than Stewart, for *Mr. Smith Goes to Washington* probably contains the finest performance of his lengthy career. It garnered the actor an Academy Award nomination, and although the 1939 Oscar went to Robert Donat for *Goodbye, Mr. Chips*, it's been said that Stewart's subsequent statuette for 1940's *The Philadelphia Story* was actually a consolation prize for the Capra classic.

James Stewart and JA in Mr. Smith Goes to Washington
(Columbia Pictures, 1939).

As in *Mr. Deeds Goes to Town*, Arthur's role is considerably smaller than her co-star's, yet vitally important, for it is her cynical but sympathetic Senatorial secretary that helps political underdog Stewart cope with his Washington adversaries and persevere against seemingly undefeatable odds.

Like *You Can't Take It With You*, this is an ensemble piece, cast to perfection with wonderful character actors such as Claude Rains, Thomas Mitchell, Edward Arnold, Beulah Bondi and Harry Carey. Although *It's a Wonderful Life* was Frank Capra's personal favorite among his movies, *Mr. Smith Goes to Washington* is quite possibly his finest achievement.

Despite the inventive nuances she customarily brought to such hero-support roles as those of her Capra pictures, Arthur's innate feminism now drove her to seek stronger women's parts, and she devoted much of her leisure time to seeking out suitable plays and stories. In a mid-1940 article entitled "The Private World of Jean Arthur," she told *Movie Mirror*'s Marion Rhea, "Being a stooge in pictures like the ones Frank Capra makes is wonderful, of course, and I'm lucky to have such an opportunity, but I'd like to play a real role."

As in 1939, Arthur had two Columbia pictures released as the new decade began: the marital comedy *Too Many Husbands* and a welcome return to the rugged outdoors for the Western *Arizona*.

Coincidentally, 1940 witnessed the release of two separate comedies with the same theme—that of an individual who remarries following the "drowning" of a spouse, only to have that original mate turn up very much alive. *Too Many Husbands*, based on the Somerset Maugham play *Home and Beauty*, teams Arthur with Melvyn Douglas as the second husband, with Fred MacMurray as the first. Directed by an uninspired Wesley Ruggles, it's a pleasantly fluffy time-passer with an ending that never quite solves its intrinsic marital dilemma.

By contrast, RKO's more successful *My Favorite Wife* trades genders to offer Irene Dunne as the "late" wife who returns to complicate the lives of husband Cary Grant and his new bride Gail Patrick. The latter script is of superior quality, and there's little doubt that Dunne and Grant will reunite. But how? In the case of *Too Many Husbands*, neither mate appears to be a prize catch, leaving audiences indifferent as to whom its heroine will end up with. One critic assessed the movie as "an unfortunate waste of talent."

Columbia Pictures continued to keep their "first lady" busy, although not always in the films for which she was announced. The 1940-1941 season was to have her star in something called *In Old New Orleans* under George Stevens' direction. The picture was never made. And *Our Wife* might have reteamed her with Melvyn Douglas, but instead featured recent Oscar-nominee Ruth Hussey.

Jean Arthur had long been self-conscious about her physical appearance on film, and that insecurity only increased with time. In the spring of 1940, cast romantically opposite 21-year-old newcomer William Holden, the 39-year-old actress first encountered him on *Arizona*'s Tucson-area desert location: looking him up and down without comment, she then walked off, leaving Holden both puzzled and uncertain of what lay ahead during production. Under the circumstances, it's surprising how well the two worked together in this pre-Civil War yarn. And, as artfully photographed by Joseph Walker, their 18-year age difference is indiscernible.

William Holden and JA in Arizona (Columbia Pictures, 1940).

Arthur plays a mannish, pie-baking pioneer, courted by restless drifter Holden, who's bound for California. She goes into the freight business, competing with crooked Porter Hall. The sprawling plot brings Holden back to marry her, but first there are complications involving cattle, Indians and a gun battle.

*Arizona* is stronger on atmosphere than character, and although Arthur plays her role with charm and conviction, it's no match for her more vivid Calamity Jane in *The Plainsman*.

The movie premiered in Tucson on Christmas Day of 1940, amid local celebrations of Pioneer Week. Uncharacteristically, Arthur attended the event, and enjoyed recounting what happened at a dinner given in her honor by the Mayor of Tucson. Preliminary to offering her a copper plate, he said: "It is indeed a pleasure to have here tonight the Sweetheart of Arizona . . . We who had the honor to know her so well came to love her . . . So, on behalf of all her most intimate friends in Arizona, I'd like to present this plate to—Miss Gene Autry!"

The indifferent quality of scripts being offered her finally moved Frank Ross to set up an independent production company to insure better movies for his wife. While Arthur was off shooting *Arizona*, he and playwright Norman Krasna were busy developing a comedy the latter had written for her called *The Devil and Miss Jones*. In conjunction with RKO, Frank Ross/Norman Krasna Productions secured popular Sam Wood (*Kitty Foyle*) to direct, assembling a topnotch cast of character actors to surround their star, including Charles Coburn, Spring Byington and Edmund Gwenn. Robert Cummings was engaged as the romantic lead, and Arthur even went so far as to pose for a bathing suit shot for publicity purposes—something she customarily hated.

*The Devil and Miss Jones* is actually less a "vehicle" for Arthur than for Coburn, who plays a wealthy department store owner who goes undercover as a shoe salesman in his store to find out who's stirring up trouble over working conditions. Arthur plays the saleswoman who unknowingly befriends the masquerading "devil," and helps humanize him, with the aid of colleague Byington and union organizer Cummings. It's all a delightful blend of script, director and enthusiastic cast, with Arthur refusing any screenplay rewrites that might have enlarged her part.

To publicize The Devil and Miss Jones, JA poses for a rare cheesecake
shot (RKO Radio Pictures, 1941).

*The Devil and Miss Jones* still plays as a delightful social comedy, but its 1941 spring release proved a box-office disappointment due, it was thought, to its unsubtle pro-union stance. With reference to the film's relative failure, Ross's son by a later marriage would report, "It absolutely devastated him." Nevertheless, Ross contracted with RKO in 1942 to produce two additional films, with his wife starring in at least one of them.

For some time, the Rosses had enjoyed the seclusion of their nine-room Brentwood home high in the Hollywood hills. In a gracious move that amazed the movie colony, *Life* magazine was permitted to photograph the ranch-style house in 1940. The accompanying interview revealed Arthur to be "a charming hostess," but little more. As she told *Life*'s attending journalist, "My personal life is my own business."

Jean Arthur so liked her Brentwood neighborhood that she purchased a nearby home for her father. Hannah Greene was by now living in Arthur's rented Carmel house, for the estrangement from husband Hubert had become permanent.

In 1942, after more than 50 years of an unhappy union, Johannah A. Greene was granted a default judgment of divorce against Hubert Sidney Greene in Monterey County, California. Two years later, the latter would die at 80. Hannah Greene went on to survive him by 15 years.

In hopes of finding a new Jean Arthur vehicle, Columbia purchased the rights to the Broadway hit comedy *My Sister Eileen* for $225,000. It was one of several projects that she was put on suspension for rejecting, and so Columbia prevented her from accepting Samuel Goldwyn's offer to re-team with Gary Cooper in *Ball of Fire* (once again, Arthur lost a role to Barbara Stanwyck). The Rosses took advantage of this hiatus in filmmaking to spend time in New York away from the movie colony.

Harry Cohn had just signed director George Stevens (*Gunga Din*) to a three—picture contract with Columbia, with the proviso that Stevens would brook no interference from the studio boss. Arthur was impressed with the filmmaker's independence, and was persuaded to co-star with Cary Grant and Ronald Colman in Stevens' *The Talk of the Town*. It would be her sole 1942 release.

The picture's intelligent Irwin Shaw-Sidney Buchman screenplay presented Arthur as a schoolteacher who rents her house to a law professor (Colman), while offering refuge to fugitive radical Grant, whom she passes off as her gardener. The movie offered an odd blend of screwball farce and social significance, and Arthur enjoyed the experience of working with the famously painstaking Stevens, who encouraged her to experiment with such bits of comic improvisation as her Katharine Hepburn-Veronica Lake impersonation.

Cary Grant, JA and Ronald Colman in The Talk of the Town
(Columbia Pictures, 1942).

Reportedly, filming *The Talk of the Town* was an enjoyable experience for all concerned, if more lucrative for its male stars: while Grant and Colman were paid upwards of $100,000 for their work, Arthur's paltry $50,000 had its roots in her ongoing cold war with Harry Cohn.

Roddy McDowall would later reflect on Jean Arthur's unique comedic talents: "She had a wonderful sense of humor, but she was a serious woman. It was her view, her slant on things that was so amusing. She just had a particular view about how to be truthful in relation to material that was good. I think that's instinctual, you can't learn that."

At a Hollywood social event, circa 1943: Frank Sinatra,
Danny Kaye and JA.

In wartime 1943, Arthur doubled her movie output with two comedies, *The More the Merrier* for Columbia, and *A Lady Takes a Chance* for her producer-husband at RKO. Frank Ross was also part of the four-man team responsible for the former's amusing script, along with Richard Flournoy, Lewis R. Foster and Robert Russell.

*The More the Merrier*, for whose original story Ross and Russell split the credit, concerns a housing shortage in wartime Washington that has Government worker Arthur sharing her spacious apartment with elderly retiree Charles Coburn, and eventually Air Force sergeant Joel McCrea, as well. She's initially engaged to dull bureaucrat Richard Gaines but, with sly cupid Coburn's machinations, finds a more suitable match with McCrea.

Charles Coburn and JA in the The More the Merrier
(Columbia Pictures, 1943).

An excellent screenplay and Stevens' witty direction make this one of the top comedies of World War II, copping a Best Supporting Actor Oscar for Coburn's endearing performance and, for Jean Arthur, her first and only Academy Award *nomination*. But the statuette that year went to the relatively unknown Jennifer Jones for *The Song of Bernadette*. Considering her many highly regarded contributions to film history, Arthur's lack of award recognition has been much discussed in books and articles over the years. Certainly, her lack of rapport with the fourth estate didn't help. In 1942, Hollywood's Women's Press Club "honored" Arthur with their annual Sour Apple Award, and columnist Hedda Hopper dubbed her "the least popular woman in Hollywood." Nor did she have many friends among Academy voters. Finally, Columbia's Harry Cohn had little interest in campaigning on her behalf for awards; she had given him just too many headaches.

*A Lady Takes a Chance* teamed the petite Arthur with big John Wayne in a romantic comedy about an Eastern tourist's attraction to a rodeo performer she meets on a bus tour of the West. Originally, Western specialist Henry Hathaway was engaged to direct the Robert Ardrey screenplay, but Arthur protested ("He'll just turn it into another fat Western!") and had him replaced with William A. Seiter, who had helmed her 1935 comedy *If You Could Only Cook* and could, therefore, be relied on to mine the script's humor.

John Wayne, JA and the production crew of A Lady Takes a Chance
(RKO Radio Pictures, 1943).

Wayne was kind enough at the time to sing his co-star's praises in a fan magazine interview, while defending her "inferiority complex." And, while there was no special off-the-set friendship, they maintained a cordial working relationship during the location shoot. It would be her last picture made in collaboration with her husband, who co-produced with his brother, Richard Ross.

With but one more picture owed Columbia on her contract, Arthur looked forward to its immediate fulfillment. On vacation in New York, she was offered a script called *The Woman Doctor*, which she refused. As she told Louella Parsons: "I couldn't play a woman doctor. To me there is something especially distasteful about working with a cadaver, and that was all in the script. It gave me chills up and down my spine."

Instead, she agreed to appear in *The Impatient Years*, an uneasy blend of comedy and drama in which she was to team for the fourth time with Joel McCrea. But the actor withdrew from the project prior to filming, and Arthur nearly followed suit, rather than accept the substitution of 29-year-old Lee Bowman. Perhaps her eagerness to complete her contract and get away from Harry Cohn altogether motivated her to accept Bowman as her leading man (based on his screen test), but their onscreen partnership failed to generate sparks. There was little that director Irving Cummings could do to help, even with the invaluable supporting presence of Charles Coburn, Edgar Buchanan, Jane Darwell and Harry Davenport.

Lee Bowman and JA in The Impatient Years
(Columbia Pictures, 1944).

In his 1967 biography *King Cohn*, Bob Thomas asserts that, upon completion of her contract, Jean Arthur ran around the Columbia lot, jubilantly yelling "I'm free! I'm free!" This may have been somewhat of an exaggeration, but she appeared to have little interest in further moviemaking, rejecting offers from Warner Bros. to film the Broadway hit *The Voice of the Turtle* (the role went to Eleanor Parker) and from 20th Century-Fox to co-star with Rex Harrison in *Anna and the King of Siam* (Irene Dunne took that part).

By this time, Frank Ross's production company had folded and so, for all intents and purposes, it seemed, had his marriage. In the spring of 1944, gossip queen Louella Parsons had predicted its demise, reporting that Arthur was now living in New York, while Ross remained in Hollywood, toiling to adapt Lloyd C. Douglas's novel *The Robe* for the screen. In the words of an unidentified friend: "Jean and Frank were always complete opposites. She loved solitude and symphony music; he loved parties, people and jazz. But they had an immensely happy marriage for a long time. It was when his interests began to turn from strict management of Jean to movie-making on his own that things went wrong." Rumors began to circulate that Arthur had chosen to retire from acting, especially after she withdrew her entry from the *Hollywood Player's Directory*, an annual compilation of working movie actors. In truth, she was merely retreating from filmmaking.

In 1945, it was announced that Jean Arthur had signed to star in Garson Kanin's Broadway comedy *Born Yesterday*, which the playwright had created with her in mind. In it she'd portray Billie Dawn, a "dumb blonde" ex-chorus girl and current junk dealer's mistress who transforms into a smart and educated woman under the tutelage of an intellectual writer named Paul Verrall.

Arthur had her reservations about certain aspects of the script, and was uncomfortable with the play's transition from outright farce to character comedy. In short, she wanted to be "ladylike" in an *un*ladylike role.

Kanin had to persuade producer Max Gordon to cast Jean Arthur in the part, because word had reached Gordon that the actress was overly shy, difficult, and a snob, qualities bound to interfere with her interpretation of the character. Finally, Gordon even accepted Arthur's unusual stipulation that, in addition to her $2,500 weekly salary and a share in the play's gross, she would have approval rights over her stage manager and publicist, plus the use of a personal maid, beautician and chauffeur.

Amid preparations for *Born Yesterday*, Frank Capra offered her the part eventually played by Donna Reed in *It's a Wonderful Life*. She turned it down, supposedly because, for some unspecified reason, she didn't want to work with James Stewart again. When *Born Yesterday* opened during its tryout in New Haven, Connecticut, on December 20, 1945, Jean Arthur charmed the critics. The praise continued with the play's subsequent engagement in Boston, where the *Herald*'s Elinor Hughes wrote: "Jean Arthur's performance should give great pleasure alike to her huge screen public and to those who have never seen her before either on the stage or in pictures. Her style of acting is easy, natural and poised, her timing excellent, and she can throw away lines as well as drive them home."

During rehearsals, Arthur had complained about what she considered vulgarities in the character and dialogue, demanding changes that Kanin, who was also directing, attempted to accommodate without compromising his work. Another of Arthur's complaints was actor Richard E. Davis, whose Paul Verrall she felt was weak and inadequate. She was assured that a replacement would be found before tryouts began. Instead, Davis continued in the role until the final performance in Boston, when Gary Merrill took over the part. It would be his one and only performance opposite Arthur, whose deteriorating health problems, whether genuine or psychosomatic, forced her out of the play altogether. In Philadelphia, the little-known Judy Holliday succeeded her and played the role for three years on Broadway. Coincidentally, Holliday went on to win an Oscar for *Born Yesterday*'s film version and at Columbia Pictures, where she soon became Harry Cohn's new queen of the lot.

Many years later, Jean Arthur reflected: "I could have played the part, but I could not have given the performance Judy Holliday gave." She also alluded to personal problems at the time, surrounding her disintegrating marriage to Frank Ross.

Arthur now agreed to team with Cary Grant in *The Bishop's Wife*, for Samuel Goldwyn, but production delays (or perhaps a second look at the script) caused her to withdraw. Loretta Young replaced her. In a puzzling move that made news and startled the movie colony, Arthur, who had never completed high school, left the West Coast in the spring of 1947 to settle temporarily in Columbia, Missouri. There she took classes at the all-female Stephens College to study such subjects as biology, geology, philosophy and the humanities. From all reports, she also enjoyed friendly relations with her fellow students, despite the considerable age gap.

Arthur remained at Stephens for only six weeks, leaving prior to graduation with the claim that financial constraints now motivated her return to filmmaking. Frank Capra entertained plans to co-star her with Bing Crosby in an adaptation of Jessamyn West's Quaker-flavored period piece *Friendly Persuasion*, but nothing materialized from that project; in the mid-Fifties it would become a William Wyler film with Gary Cooper and Dorothy McGuire.

Instead, Jean Arthur accepted a three-picture contract to return to her old stamping grounds at Paramount, beginning with Billy Wilder's *A Foreign Affair*. Arthur saw to it that she received top billing, above the title and ahead of her teammates, Marlene Dietrich and John Lund. It did not endear her to her German colleague.

This was a Charles Brackett-Billy Wilder screenplay set in postwar Berlin, to which bespectacled, prudish Iowa Congresswoman Arthur flies as part of a committee inspecting the morals and morale of U. S. occupation forces. Dietrich plays a nightclub singer and suspected Nazi collaborator enjoying the protection of an American officer, whose identity Arthur's determined to uncover. Enlisting the aid of Army Captain Lund, a fellow Iowan, she finds herself falling in love with him, little suspecting that he is actually Dietrich's protector.

The women were especially well cast in this popular film, with the incredibly glamorous Dietrich stealing much of the attention from Arthur's plain-Jane character. The latter's best scene is that in which, awkwardly attired for a night out on the town, and mellowed by a couple of drinks, she cuts loose with "The Iowa Corn Song."

As Congresswoman Phoebe Frost in A Foreign Affair
(Paramount Pictures, 1948).

During production, there was no love lost between Dietrich and Arthur, who deeply resented the German-speaking rapport between her co-star and Wilder, whom she blamed for favoring Dietrich at her own expense. Forty years later, after a television viewing of *A Foreign Affair*, Arthur finally made amends with her director by calling him to report that she "absolutely loved" the movie, asking whether they could still be friends.

With the June 1948 release of *A Foreign Affair*, Jean Arthur ended a nearly four-year gap between pictures, and her appearance was, at 47 (or 39 by her count), very much that of a middle-aged woman. Both critics and audiences seemed pleased to welcome her back. While lavishing greater praise on Dietrich, the *New York Times'* Bosley Crowther opined, "Jean Arthur is beautifully droll as the prim and punctilious Congresswoman who has her eyes popped open by the power of love."

The Jean Arthur-Frank Ross marriage officially ended in early 1949, when she filed for divorce. According to her friend Pete Ballard, the actress had considered the union a happy one until, in 1945, she found in her car a woman's scarf that turned out to belong to Paramount contract player Joan Caulfield, with whom Ross was involved. Their final decree was granted on March 22, 1950, and five weeks later he and Caulfield were wed. Their union would last 10 years.

On April 24, 1950, Arthur returned triumphantly to Broadway in *Peter Pan*, portraying the "boy who wouldn't grow up" of James M. Barrie's play that she had so long wanted to enact. This semi-musical revival (music and lyrics by Leonard Bernstein) didn't require the actress to sing, but it did cast her opposite the Captain Hook/Mr. Darling of movie bogeyman Boris Karloff. Part of its lifelong appeal to her was what she deemed the play's philosophy: "It means nonconformity and freedom of the imagination and the individual. I think that's what Barrie meant."

As Peter Pan with Mary Martin at a costume party held at Hollywood's
West Side Tennis Club (author's collection).

Jean Arthur and her close friend Mary Martin had long talked about their mutual desire to play Peter, and it was Martin who was initially approached about this revival. At that time, she was busy starring in the hit musical *South Pacific*, which prompted producer Peter Lawrence to seek out Vera

Zorina, whose husband, Goddard Lieberson, promised financial backing for the show. However, production delays discouraged Zorina, and it was only after her withdrawal that Arthur's name was submitted by agent Maynard Morris.

In an effort to convince herself that, at 49, she could play an adolescent boy, Arthur rented Broadway's Royale Theatre and performed so impressive an audition for Lawrence that the role was undeniably hers. Indeed, so eager was she to realize her lifelong dream that she offered to help finance the production, as well as participate in a number of backers' auditions.

Arthur was adamant about her personal conception of Peter, chopping her hair short and refusing the tailored costume especially designed for her. Instead, she wore an outfit of her own making, consisting of tights, a shabby, matching jersey and moccasins. The last thing she wanted was the cute, elflike appearance of past Peter Pans.

As the title role in the 1950 Broadway production of Peter Pan
(author's collection).

In the show's Playbill, Arthur refused to permit anything beyond a short, five-line listing that identified her as "one of the best-known actresses on the American screen," and listing *Mr. Smith Goes to Washington* as her all-time favorite movie.

Jean Arthur reportedly played Peter Pan as "a cocky, matter-of-fact boy." In the *Times*, Brooks Atkinson typified the New York critics with his praise: "When you think of how arch and maudlin the part might be in less scrupulous hands, you can appreciate the ease and simplicity of her performance."

Rave reviews prompted sell-out houses, and *Peter Pan* appeared set for a long and successful run. By midsummer, the toll of eight performances a week in so energetic a role was tiring the star, and she requested an immediate month-long vacation that producer Lawrence balked at. First, a "star" replacement would have to be found, and Shirley Temple was briefly considered. In her autobiography, Temple recounts how Arthur phoned her, begging her, "Don't take Peter Pan away from me, please!" Finally, on last—minute notice, 23-year-old understudy Barbara Baxley had to take over the part, even though she had yet to master the flying and the fencing.

The press were given "laryngitis" as the cause of Arthur's withdrawal, but when she produced a doctor's certificate recommending she rest through at least another two-and-a-half weeks, producer Lawrence took the matter to Actors' Equity, planning to replace Arthur with Betty Field. Finally, a deal was struck to let Arthur have a total of two weeks off to rest, while Baxley played Peter. Upon her return, Arthur insisted that Baxley accept her check for a thousand dollars, leading to a lifelong friendship between them.

Those involved have conjectured whether Jean Arthur's erratic behavior actually stemmed from fatigue, illness or undisclosed personal problems, perhaps involving Frank Ross. However, she returned to the play and remained professional throughout the remainder of its run, which concluded on January 27, 1951, with a record-setting 321 performances.

Marcia Henderson and JA in the 1950 Broadway production of Peter Pan (author's collection).

Several days later, *Peter Pan* began a road tour in Boston, continuing on through other cities until, on April 14th in Chicago, Arthur was forced to leave the show to fulfill a contractual agreement with Paramount. The studio had allowed her a year off for the play, but now required her back for the George Stevens Western *Shane*. This time, Joan McCracken replaced Arthur as Peter, resulting in an immediate downturn at the box-office. The show closed two weeks later in Minneapolis.

In retrospect, Jean Arthur considered *Peter Pan* the apex of her stage and screen career: "That was my happiest role and I think my finest acting."

In the words of longtime Arthur friend Nell Eurich: "That role changed her life. From then on, she began to wear her hair like Peter Pan. She lived that role."

With its story set in 1889 Wyoming, *Shane* was filmed entirely on location in and around picturesque Jackson Hole. It would be Jean Arthur's first Technicolor movie—and her last experience with filmmaking. Her co-stars were diminutive tough guy Alan Ladd and her long-ago stage colleague from *The Bride of Torozko*, Van Heflin. But Arthur's favorite was the young actor cast as her son, the lively nine-year-old Brandon De Wilde, with whom she formed a close bond during production.

This now-classic tale centers on ordinary homesteaders victimized by a cattle baron and his hired guns who meet their match in a quick-triggered drifter named Shane (played by Ladd). Heflin and Arthur portrayed the central pioneer family, and although hers wasn't a large role, the actress makes every scene count, especially in the subtle, unspoken affection evident between her character and that of the charismatic Shane, before he rides off alone. Attired in a curly blonde wig and a none-too-glamorous wardrobe, Arthur appears far younger than her 50 years.

As Marian Starrett in Shane
(Paramount Pictures, 1953).

Completed in October 1951, *Shane* was not seen by the public until April 1953, due to director Stevens' painstaking post-production work on the film's editing, which only added to the budget's overrun. To recoup its losses, Paramount unsuccessfully attempted selling the movie to RKO's Howard Hughes before accepting defeat—and ultimately finding that they had a highly respected hit on their hands.

Jean Arthur harbored no fondness for *Shane*. In a 1965 interview with columnist Hedda Hopper, she recalled, "I didn't like it because I couldn't use any comedy bits at all—just had to act old and worn out." No wonder, then, that when she walked off the set after the final day of shooting, she did so without the customary words of thanks or farewell to anyone.

After *Shane*, Arthur still owed Paramount two more films, but as she systematically rejected all the scripts offered her, the studio finally terminated their deal by paying her $200,000, about one quarter of what she would have earned for a pair of movies.

Next to Peter Pan, the legendary figure that most intrigued Jean Arthur was Joan of Arc, especially in the George Bernard Shaw play *Saint Joan*. Her affinity for that role was later explained in a 1966 *New York Times* interview: "I love Joan. She was a nonconformist too, a believer in her own intuition. Intuition, that's what Joan's voices were. She never killed anybody. She just wanted everyone to go home and mind their own business."

JA and Van Heflin in Shane (Paramount Pictures, 1953).

In the summer of 1954, Arthur engaged the services of theatrical agent Helen Harvey, and gained an introduction to Broadway producer Robert Whitehead, whom she approached about reviving *Saint Joan* for her. The plan involved a 30-week tour that would begin in September and arrive on Broadway the following April for a limited engagement. The large supporting cast included such reliable actors as Arthur's *Bride of Torozko* co-star Sam Jaffe, Paul Richards, George Macready and Frank Silvera.

Unfortunately, Jean Arthur enjoyed no rapport with her director, the veteran Harold Clurman, whose originally-agreed-upon concept apparently fell apart during rehearsals. In a 1972 *New York Times* interview, she remembered: "Afterward he forgot all about our agreement. He ordered me to stand on the stage and not to move, and then he directed the actors to ignore me. 'Just recite the language,' he'd say to me, 'and that will be enough.'"

Since Arthur had director approval, she came to regret not having had Clurman fired. As Helen Harvey recalled: "He humiliated her in front of the company, belittled her, just destroyed any little self-confidence she had. I was surprised he didn't realize how vulnerable she was. I think everybody else in the cast realized it."

*Saint Joan* opened in Wilmington, Delaware, on September 17, 1954, to an enthusiastic reception from both press and audience. Amid the tour, Clurman's criticism of his star persisted, although the local newspaper critics gave her favorable notices.

As Joan of Arc in the ill-fated 1954 stage tour of Saint Joan
(author's collectiion).

By the time the company arrived in Chicago that November for a three-week engagement, a familiar Jean Arthur health pattern had surfaced. So upset was she with the continuing directorial criticism, in addition to what she considered her personal failure to achieve perfection in a role she loved, that doctors finally diagnosed "complete exhaustion." She was ordered to take at least a month's rest. "And that was the end of *Saint Joan*," the actress later reflected, "the play I had wanted to do all my life."

A dispute followed between the star and producer Whitehead, who never forgave the manner in which she left the play. The matter was submitted to Actors' Equity for arbitration, but any punitive action against Arthur was averted when her friend Barbara Baxley intervened on her behalf, confirming that Arthur's "illness" was genuine.

Other factors may have contributed to Jean Arthur's ill-health at the time: the I.R.S. claimed that she owed hundreds of thousands in back taxes from 1942 to 1947 (connected to Frank Ross's production company); nor was she happy with the success of her old pal Mary Martin in the hit Broadway musical version of *Peter Pan*. Eventually, Ross's considerable profits from *The Robe* helped solve Arthur's financial woes, but nothing could erase her severe disappointments about *Saint Joan*: "When the show folded, I folded. I'd put everything into *Saint Joan*. There was nothing left . . . I felt like the walking maimed."

For a time, she visited with her East Coast friends Nell and Alvin Eurich, and then returned to California and "Driftwood," her house in Carmel, where Hannah Greene had been living for some time. There, the actress would embrace a certain measure of seclusion, while forming friendships with a select few who would honor her privacy. Interviewed years later by Arthur biographer John Oller, some of those friends fondly remembered enjoyable times with her, while also recalling the actress' moodiness and bouts of erratic behavior. One pal termed her "a seagull, just flying with the breeze, flowing with the currents." Recalled another, "She never stopped being Peter Pan. She had the attention span of a four-year-old."

In 1959, when an unexpected visitor identified himself as a reporter and requested an interview, she responded: "Well, you just get on the other side of that fence. I don't mean to be impolite to you personally, but I'm out of the business and all I want to do is read and be let alone."

For some time, Hannah Greene had been bedridden in the aftermath of a stroke and a broken hip, and that incapacitation drew mother and daughter closer together than heretofore. Arthur had the help of a maid and, on occasion, her aunt Pearl, who visited her half-sister periodically. But all of that came to an end on December 4, 1959, when Mrs. Greene died at 88. On the night of her passing, according to an unidentified friend, Jean Arthur "turned up the hi-fi as high as it would go and turned on every light in the house. Her mother passed away in a shout of glory."

After having her mother's remains cremated and the ashes scattered at sea, the actress arranged to have the local newspaper simply report that Johannah Greene was survived by her son Donald Greene of Santa Cruz, and daughter Gladys Greene of Carmel.

In the wake of her mother's death, aunt Pearl stayed on in Carmel to keep her niece company—until they had a falling out when the older woman decided to leave a few days earlier than planned for a return visit to Montana. Reportedly, the two women never saw each other again.

Shortly before her mother's death, Arthur had met Ellen Mastroianni, the neighbor of a friend she was visiting. Not only did they share an interest in dogs, but the other woman had little knowledge of or interest in show business, and was quite indifferent to Jean Arthur's fame. Their personalities couldn't have been more diverse, and yet the two soon became inseparable friends. Arthur was then nearly 60, while Mastroianni, an unmarried Army nurse, was 45. Rallying from her post-*Saint Joan* "down period" under this new relationship, Arthur now blossomed and co-hosted house parties, entertaining friends and eventually considering a return to acting.

In 1961, she reportedly was set to join the cast of *Act One*, the film adaptation of Moss Hart's autobiographical best-seller, to be directed by Joshua Logan. But when the latter was replaced by Dore Schary, Arthur lost interest in the project. The following year, producer Jerry Wald initially wanted her for the mother in William Inge's play *A Loss of Roses*, but that 1963 film, when released as *The Stripper*, featured Claire Trevor in the part. It was reported that, after reading the screenplay, Jean Arthur felt that the role was too serious.

A project that held greater interest for her was Paul Gallico's charming novella *Mrs. 'Arris Goes to Paris*, and her desire to portray that cockney charwoman moved her to option the story as a vehicle for herself. At the time, she hoped to persuade George Stevens to direct. But her enthusiasm waned, and she later sold the rights. With Angela Lansbury in the role, that project eventually became a 1992 movie for television.

Instead, Jean Arthur returned her attention to the as-yet-unfulfilled effort to portray Joan of Arc. This time, the result was a staged reading of Shaw's *Saint Joan*, given 10 performances at the University of California's 150-seat Durham Studio Theater at Berkeley in February 1964. With Arthur in the title role (at 63, it was somewhat of a stretch to enact that youthful character), the play was rehearsed and advertised without any mention of its celebrity guest-star. With a cast filled out by graduate students and faculty members, there was no scenery and no traditional period costuming, although its leading lady chose to wear a black leotard beneath a red leather uniform indicative of her character.

Just prior to the play's opening, a San Francisco columnist leaked the news of Jean Arthur's involvement in the production, with the not-unexpected result that the entire run immediately sold out, with dozens of others turned away. The newsworthy event also guaranteed critical coverage. The San Francisco *Chronicle* called her Joan "exquisitely original," while the *Examiner*'s critic observed that "the mystic, the martyr, the saint and the innocent were missing," but "the earthy, intense peasant girl was there." In a way, her success at Berkeley helped obliterate the unpleasant memories of that *Saint Joan* production a decade earlier.

Television was not a medium that held much interest for Arthur. Nor did she even own a set in 1964 when Lucille Ball tried to interest her in making her TV debut on *The Lucy Show*, for which a script was especially devised. Although this plan failed to work out to Arthur's satisfaction, Ball's continued enthusiasm about the medium encouraged the older actress to take the unusual step (for her) of engaging a manager, Eddie Dukoff, to seek an appropriate TV property for her. The result was an episode of the durable *Gunsmoke* series, entitled "Thursday's Child," that ran on March 6, 1965. In this Arthur-tailored story, she portrayed the mother of a young outlaw sought for murder. When the fugitive's wife dies in childbirth, he attempts a getaway, using the baby as a shield, and Arthur is forced to shoot him down, to prevent further bloodshed.

James Arness and JA in the "Thursday's Child" episode of Gunsmoke
(CBS-TV, March 6, 1965).

Although she refused any pre-show interviews for the CBS telecast, her guest appearance was suitably advertised and drew high ratings, as well as laudatory reviews. Arthur enjoyed the whole process of working in TV, and termed it "a kind of opening of a door."

With her interest in acting reinforced, Arthur now considered a return to feature filmmaking in 1965 with Columbia's offer to star in a project called *Life With Mother Superior*, to be directed by Ida Lupino. Perhaps a read-through of the screenplay dissuaded her, for she ultimately rejected the idea. Once again, Rosalind Russell replaced her in a movie that was released in 1966 as *The Trouble With Angels*.

Dukoff tried to interest Arthur in performing several scenes from *Peter Pan* for TV, but she declined, stating her preference for *Saint Joan*. The customarily age-conscious actress didn't seem to realize that, at 65, the notion of playing a legendary teenager on such a close-up medium might not have been a wise one. Or perhaps her head had been turned by the *Hollywood Reporter*'s critic, who wrote of her *Gunsmoke* appearance, "she looked as pretty, pert and youthful as ever."

What did finally capture Jean Arthur's imagination was a proposal by writer Jay Richard Kennedy to fashion a TV comedy series for her, focusing on a sort of female Perry Mason figure, a woman lawyer with an offbeat approach to her profession. Arthur immediately embraced the idea, and a deal was made with Universal Television to turn out a half-hour show, with the sponsorship of General Foods, entitled *Mother's Word Is Law*. With the first episode scheduled to air in September, shooting on the pilot was set to begin in June of 1966.

Arthur's professional enthusiasm now motivated her to focus on her physical appearance with an intensity that she'd not known earlier. For the first time, she underwent plastic surgery on her face and arms, and then submitted to the regimentation of a noted health spa. Finally, she took to swimming morning laps in an unheated pool, negotiating a contractual stipulation that she wouldn't have to work past 5:30, when she might be de-energized.

JA displays great form to publicize The Jean Arthur Show
(CBS-TV,1966).

For *The Jean Arthur Show*, as it was now less imaginatively called, she was outfitted in a stylish Nolan Miller wardrobe, with her white, mannish haircut covered with a fashionable blonde wig. As she remarked at the time: "I didn't want to come back as a character actress. I think that must be heartbreaking. I love to play comedy, and character parts couldn't be fun. I suppose I love being the big shot."

During the show's production period, Arthur and her friend Ellen Mastroianni rented a house in nearby Laurel Canyon. Uncharacteristically, the actress lent her spare time to promoting the series, with interview-based articles appearing prominently in both *TV Guide* and the *New York Times*. Former actor Richard Quine directed the pilot episode with great care and, to insure public interest, CBS engaged such popular guest-stars as Ray Bolger, Wally Cox and Mickey Rooney.

Richard Conte and JA in the pilot episode of The Jean Arthur Show
(CBS-TV, 1966).

Some thought the network's scheduling of *The Jean Arthur Show* in the 10 p.m. slot on Monday nights was a mistake. But perhaps a bigger mistake was postponing the original pilot episode to air the Rooney one first. Corporate thinking reasoned that his star power would insure the premiere's success. Witnessing a situation comedy virtually without laughs, the *New York Times* was more kind than critical: "The plot was far-fetched rather than funny, and Miss Arthur's part was virtually subordinate to that of Mickey Rooney."

To make it worse, the sitcom was accompanied by a laugh-track that only emphasized its lack of genuine humor. Producer Si Rose later recalled Arthur's loss of interest in the wake of the reviews: "From then on, she was very tense and felt kind of betrayed, like we had lulled her into a false sense of security." Apparently, she now attempted to be more hands-on and was less cooperative, rejecting script suggestions. A month after its premiere, CBS announced the show's cancellation, which concluded with the pilot on December 5th. It was the twelfth episode to air.

In a November issue of *TV Guide*, Jean Arthur spoke frankly about her sitcom with writer Frank DeRoos: "I'm terribly disappointed, of course, because I love the work so much. But I wouldn't want to face another one of those scripts. We knew about the third show that I was playing straight man, and we tried to do something about it. But here is the other side—a bunch of fellows at Universal who have a budget. There wasn't anybody brave enough to say 'Let's quit until we can find a way'."

If there had been an effort on the part of the sitcom's scriptwriters to recapture the popular Jean Arthur big-screen persona of 25 years earlier, the results proved unsuccessful. In the light of Lucille Ball's great TV popularity, perhaps the general expectation was that any other TV comedy actress would be a Lucy clone. That same season, the unique Tammy Grimes met a failure similar to Arthur's with the cancellation of *The Tammy Grimes Show*.

As for her future plans, Arthur told *TV Guide*: "I'm going back to Carmel. I have a beautiful house up there, and I've got four cats that I am lonesome for."

Retreating to Carmel, as usual, helped heal the disappointments of her most recent foray into the entertainment world, and the quiet life by the sea now helped Jean Arthur heal her wounds in the company of her friends and animals. Her peaceful existence there was sadly interrupted on April 4, 1967, when she received the news that her brother Don, a nursing home resident at the Carmel Convalescent Hospital, had ended his own life in a bathtub wrist-slashing. So estranged were the siblings by this time that a newspaper death notice listed him as having "no known survivors." Without publicity, Arthur arranged for his cremation and ocean burial.

That spring, Arthur's professional spirits were temporarily lifted when Broadway producer Cheryl Crawford phoned her about a new play for which she thought the actress might be well-suited. Richard Chandler's *The Freaking Out of Stephanie Blake* centered on an independent-minded Midwesterner who arrives in New York's Greenwich Village to "save" her willful niece from surrendering to the hippie lifestyle, yet ends up joining the movement and becoming a free spirit herself.

Arthur had based her acceptance of the project on a reading of only the first scene of the as-yet-unfinished play, which had impressed her: "Most of the plays people send me are about the past. This one is about today, and I believe in what it's saying. I didn't want to do any of the formula plays, which are boring to me, because we are in a great evolutionary and revolutionary period."

In signing Arthur to a contract, Crawford was assured that her star's unreliable behavior patterns were "a thing of the past," and that she had been "most cooperative" during production of *The Jean Arthur Show*. Anxious to work in the theatre once again, she arrived in Manhattan, accompanied by Ellen Mastroianni, in the late summer of 1967, and settled into the upscale Hampshire House on Central Park South.

Under the direction of 28-year-old John Hancock, rehearsals began with a large cast of mostly-unknowns. Jean Arthur's was the play's only "name," and so it was considered vital that everything proceed to her satisfaction. Co-producers Cheryl Crawford and Carl Schaeffer assured her that they would honor her ideas about script changes. Unfortunately, Arthur had not seen a completed work before signing, and her enthusiastic reaction to the offer was merely based on promises. During rehearsals, she suggested many alterations, few of which were made. Arthur would later recall: "We kept getting new scenes every day, and you wouldn't believe how stupid they were. They *couldn't* have been written by the person who wrote that first scene. I'd like to find out some day who *did* write that scene."

Ultimately, *The Freaking Out of Stephanie Blake* proved a complete disaster. Director Hancock quit the show, and was replaced by Michael Kahn, necessitating additional rehearsal time and even moved Arthur to contribute an investment of $25,000 to keep things on track. Preview performances were cancelled, and then re-scheduled, and the play's opening postponed from October to November. On the matinee performance of Wednesday, November 2nd, Arthur made her entrance out of character, ignoring the other actors by walking to the stage apron and directly addressing the audience with an impromptu monologue encompassing the play and her affection for her fellow actors, and concluding with the comment "I just can't go on." To which producer Crawford, standing at the back of the theatre, shouted back, "You will go on! You will play the play!"

And so, begging the audience's indulgence with regard to her failing voice, Jean Arthur went offstage and began again. Projecting in little more than a heavy whisper, she proceeded through the performance. At the play's conclusion, according to cast member Barton Heyman, waving her hands in the air in a farewell gesture, "She sort of floated out, and that was the last I saw of her."

Jean Arthur, it seemed, had retreated to her hotel room and could not be reached directly. Cheryl Crawford sent her a telegram that read "your failure to appear . . . will necessitate the closing of the play . . . with an estimated loss of $250,000." Arthur's manager, Eddie Dukoff, countered with a telegram stating that the star was under a doctor's care, but hoped that, after a three-day rest of her voice, she'd be able to return for the play's opening night. But the premiere had to be cancelled and three days later *The Freaking Out of Stephanie Blake* was officially dead.

As to what went wrong, opinions varied widely. Some thought it was the play's author, while others blamed the directors. One cast member, Franklin Cover, termed it "The weirdest experience I ever had," while actress Dena Dietrich told Arthur biographer John Oller: "Most of us in the production felt that it was inconceivable that this kind of thing could happen. I felt sorry for her, but more for us, who were left out of work."

Through the suggestion of her friend Nell Eurich, who had recently become dean of faculty at Vassar College in Poughkeepsie, N.Y., Jean Arthur found a new outlet for her artistic creativity as a drama teacher there. Moving to upstate New York, she began as a class observer whose opinion was occasionally sought by William Rothwell, who taught freshman acting. Eventually, she would officially share teaching responsibilities with the younger and more dynamic Clint Atkinson. Many students thought Arthur's approach "corny." One student, Robyn Reeves Travers, later recalled: "The things she had done on film seemed rather dated to us. The gee-whiz Americana (of *Mr. Smith Goes to Washington*) was out of favor in 1969."

William Rothwell was more specific about Jean Arthur's academic shortcomings: "She was very good at criticism; she could put her finger on exactly what was wrong with the interpretation of the role, and then she would show them how she thought it should be done. But the problem was that she could not elicit from the student a performance on her own."

Although she kept a low profile as Jean Arthur, the actress is well remembered by her former students as a unique personality, always attired in pants and with her hair kept short. As Nancy Barber remembers Arthur: "My impression of her was Peter Pan. She was very childlike in her mannerisms, and completely optimistic about what she did."

In 1972, after four years at the college, it was time for a change. As she stated at the time: "I'm very grateful to Vassar for giving me the chance to prove that I have something to contribute to young people. But I'm lonely here. The faculty is quite conservative, and I can count the teachers with whom I have some communications on my hands and still have some fingers left over. I'm ready for something different now. I'm ready for some excitement."

Whatever "excitement" Jean Arthur had in mind, it didn't include a return to filmmaking. During this period she rejected Hollywood offers to bring her back before moviegoers in both the musical remake of *Lost Horizon* and *Junior Bonner*, in roles eventually played by Liv Ullmann and Ida Lupino.

Surprisingly, Arthur responded (albeit with some reluctance) to an invitation to participate in a tribute to Frank Capra, sponsored by the USA Film Festival at Southern Methodist University in Dallas. Eschewing the celebratory parties and remaining secluded in her hotel room, the actress quietly attended the initial screening, *Mr. Deeds Goes to Town*, with the director persuading her to join him onstage to an ovation. When she realized how much the youthful audience adored her, she blossomed, commenting afterwards, "It was just the most fun I've ever had." And, for the rest of the week's tribute, she happily accompanied Capra in post-screening discussions of *You Can't Take It With You* and *Mr. Smith Goes to Washington*.

Publicist John Springer, who was present during the SMU tribute, subsequently tried to secure Arthur's participation in his series of "Legendary Ladies" evenings at New York's Town Hall. At first Arthur agreed, but then withdrew. Facing a Manhattan audience to accompany film clips with a question-and-answer segment proved psychologically daunting for her. Instead, she relished a return to the academic world and a chance to *direct*.

And so Jean Arthur next accepted an offer to join the drama faculty of the North Carolina School of the Arts in Winston-Salem. From all later reports, the actress was not a good teacher, for she had trouble imparting her knowledge to the students. Beverly Petty, who studied with Arthur as a sophomore, later described her as "a rather bitter woman," who "could treat people very badly." However, Petty thought Arthur "had a wonderful sense of humor when she wasn't being crabby or unhappy."

However, during the academic year's first semester, Arthur's drama class rebelled, demanding their freedom. Beverly Petty was one of four who remained supportive of their instructor: "Whatever Arthur's deficiencies as a teacher, she was not an evil woman. She was eccentric enough and sad enough, but she was an interesting lady. When she was charming she was charming, and when she wasn't we just cut out."

Jean Arthur returned to Carmel during the Christmas break, and was inclined to remain there until persuaded to finish out the school year by English instructor Pete Ballard, her one true friend at the school. As Ballard remembers, "she didn't have a regular class. It was more ad-hoc. They wound up letting her do a little one-act play, *Sneaky Fitch*. It was silly and nonsense, but the kids did it. But everybody just sort of cast her off."

With little in the way of campus responsibilities, Arthur now spent most of her time in her apartment with her cats, reportedly consoling herself with alcohol. Drinking may have had something to do with her arrest on March 31, 1973, in an incident involving her repeated attentions to a neighborhood dog she felt was being neglected by its owners. Despite giving police an assumed name, it soon became national news when her identity was revealed, resulting in celebrity support, both moral and financial. By the end of term, she had returned to Carmel.

That summer, Jean Arthur made her first-and-only appearance on a TV talk show when she was invited to join Frank Capra on the syndicated *Merv Griffin Show*. With the accompanying support of pals Pete Ballard and Ellen Mastroianni, Arthur handled herself well, dealing calmly with questions about the canine incident, and expressing her political views with unexpected humor.

Once again, Jean Arthur seemed to have retreated into secluded retirement. And yet her apparent urge to perform resurfaced when *Inherit the Wind* playwrights Jerome Lawrence and Robert E. Lee induced her to portray the then-fictional first woman to become Supreme Court Justice in their comedy *First Monday in October*, opposite Melvyn Douglas. Her co-star in the 1940 movie *Too Many Husbands* and somewhat ailing at 74, Douglas had to be persuaded. The play was scheduled to begin a pre-Broadway try-out on October 17, 1975 at Ohio's Cleveland Play House, before moving to Washington's Kennedy Center, and thence to New York.

Playwright Lawrence had carefully tailored the role for Arthur, whom he'd gotten to know and like personally, and although suitably warned by Garson Kanin and Cheryl Crawford, he was willing to proceed with his desired casting. On that, co-author Lee was in accord. For this play, Arthur took the situation seriously, working on her lines with Ballard and confining her alcoholic intake to one drink per day.

In Cleveland, all was not serene with the start of rehearsals that September. Arthur found reason to complain about her accommodations, her food and her costumes for the play. "I won't wear a dress," she insisted. "I want to wear pants all the way through." And despite the protestations of co-author/director Lawrence, she adamantly stuck to pantsuits for her character. For most of the cast, made up of members of the Play House resident company, Jean Arthur remained a stand-offish enigma. As for Melvyn Douglas, everyone liked him and admired his performance except Arthur. Having arrived with her role well prepared, she had little patience with Douglas' difficulty in remembering his lines. Nevertheless, it was agreed that their leading man was giving an exemplary performance, and the scenes between the two stars were well-matched. In advance of its October opening, the limited run was a sellout.

Melvyn Douglas and JA in the 1975 Cleveland Play House production of First Monday in October (author's collection).

Everyone had high hopes for opening night, a black-tie affair timed to celebrate the Play House's 60th anniversary, which happened to coincide with Arthur's 75th birthday, although she'd never admit to the fact.

As Lawrence recollected the night, "She was very down. She didn't give a performance at all. She kind of walked through it." Unfortunately, the play's opening and its star-power was sufficient to attract national attention. The reviewer from *Time* magazine thought little of the play, with his major criticism reserved for Jean Arthur: "She still has the raspy little girl's voice that people remember . . . and a spunky air of perennial optimism. But the stage has never been her home, and it is not now."

Lawrence recalls that her work improved with subsequent performances. However, the old self-doubts returned to undermine her acting. As in the past, her health deteriorated and, by the end of October, she was coughing throughout the evening. On the 30th, she sought professional advice from doctors who diagnosed her condition as a viral infection.

With no official understudy for the role, the producers desperately turned to 20-year-old Dee Hoty, who had attended to Arthur's needs and filled in during her absences at rehearsals. Not only did this willing novice save the evening, but as fellow-cast-member Eugene Hare recalls, "Dee made sense out of the play, I think, for the first time."

Because Equity rules required a union member in the role, resident actress Edith Owen soon took over and continued to fulfill the play's four-week run, which ended on November 17th. *First Monday in October* eventually reached Broadway two years later in a successful, revised edition that starred Henry Fonda and Jane Alexander.

As for Jean Arthur, she remained for a week at the Cleveland Clinic before returning to California. And, for those at the Play House there were no goodbyes. Cast member Allan Leatherman recalled that director Lawrence "handled her with kid gloves," concluding, "She just lacked self-confidence at the end. It was a pity."

Financial constraints now forced Arthur to sell her beloved Driftwood, which she'd owned since 1946. To avoid heavy capital-gains taxation she was advised to purchase a new and smaller house, then turn over that property to a pair of charities at a bargain price. A suitable dwelling was found in the vicinity, as well as within walking distance of her friend Ellen Mastroianni. And, once again, Arthur had a view of the Pacific. Eventually, she'd give up driving and rely on her friends to get around.

Now financially stabilized, Jean Arthur enjoyed her eighties in retirement. For stimulation, she had her cats and her gardens, as well as her reading, which embraced the intellectual writings of anthropologist Loren Eiseley and Jesuit theologian and paleontologist Pierre Teilhard de Chardin.

The reclusive actress had become noted for her aversion to the past, refusing any and all efforts to interview or photograph her. She didn't answer fan mail, and when the American Film Institute bestowed its Life Achievement Award on Frank Capra in 1982, she was among his few surviving stars not present. As the director then observed to the *Washington Post*'s Tom Shales: "She doesn't do very well in crowds, and she doesn't do very well with people, and she doesn't do very well with life. But she does very well as an actress."

In 1982, her ex-husband Frank Ross, now divorced from his third wife, called Arthur to inquire whether he might pay her a visit. And despite years of badmouthing him to her friends, she accepted his dinner invitation. Unexpectedly, this led to periodic get-togethers with Ross and his 12-year-old son Zan, of whom Arthur became very fond.

The 1980s brought Jean Arthur renewed notice as an actress with video releases of her classic films, as well as books like James Harvey's *Romantic Comedy* and Ed Sikov's *Screwball*. In early 1989, she surprised friend

Roddy McDowall by permitting the publication of two photos he'd taken of her in his book *Double Exposure: Take Two*.

On May 25, 1989, Jean Arthur suffered a fall, breaking her hip and causing a stroke that left her a brain-damaged invalid. Ellen Mastroianni became her fulltime caretaker from then on. Eventually, the costs of 24-hour home care necessitated transferring the actress to the Carmel Convalescent Hospital where, like her brother Don 24 years earlier, she lost her will to live. When she died at the age of 90 on June 19, 1991, heart failure was listed as the cause. In a now-established pattern familiar to members of the Greene family, there was no funeral service. Instead, cremation was followed by the scattering of her ashes at sea—off of California's Point Lobos—as carried out by Ellen Mastroianni. In her will, Arthur left her entire estate to her financial advisor, banker Peter Wright; Mastroianni had impressed upon her that *she* didn't need the money.

Frank Ross had died following brain surgery the previous year, paving the way for a sadly ironic coincidence: both of his first two wives followed him 16 months later. Just a day before Jean Arthur's passing, death had also claimed Joan Caulfield of cancer in Los Angeles. She was 69.

Without doubt, Jean Arthur lived life on her own terms. And, as exemplified by her legacy of classic film performances, she was indisputably an original.

## ##

# THE FILMS

## (in order of release)

### Somebody Lied

(Fox Film Corp., 1923) Two reels.
Directors: Stephen Roberts and Bryan Foy.
*The Film:* Jean Arthur co-starred with future cowboy star Ken Maynard in this comedy short.

### Cameo Kirby

(Fox Film Corp., 1923) Seven reels.
Director: John Ford. Scenario: Robert N. Lee. Based on the play by Booth Tarkington and Harry Leon Wilson. Cinematographer: George Schneiderman.
Cast: John Gilbert (Cameo Kirby); Gertrude Olmstead (Adele Randall); Alan Hale (Colonel Moreau); Eric Mayne (Colonel Randall); William E. Lawrence (Tom Randall); Richard Tucker (Cousin Aaron Randall); Phillips Smalley (Judge Playdell); Jack McDonald (Larkin Bunce); Jean Arthur (Ann Playdell); Eugenie Ford (Madame Davezac).
*The Film: Cameo Kirby* was the Fox remake of a popular story filmed by Paramount's Cecil B. DeMille in 1914, starring Dustin Farnum. In 1923, it became a vehicle for Fox's rising star John Gilbert, and would be an early talkie for that studio in 1930, when it featured J. Harold Murray opposite Norma Terris, with Myrna Loy in the supporting role of the heroine's friend, played here by Jean Arthur. Despite having a strong director in John Ford and seasoned fellow-players, Arthur failed to make any strong impression.

As Ann Playdell in Cameo Kirby (Fox Film Corp., 1923).

### The Temple of Venus

(Fox Film Corp., 1923) Seven reels.
Director: Henry Otto. Scenario: Henry Otto and Catherine Carr. Cinematographer: Joseph August.

*Cast:* William Walling (*Dennis Dean*); Mary Philbin (*Moira*); Micky McBain (*Micky*); Alice Day (*Peggy*); David Butler (*Nat Harper*); William Boyd (*Stanley Dale*); Phyllis Haver (*Constance Lane*); Leon Barry (*Phil Greyson*); Celeste Lee (*Venus*); Señorita Consuela (Thetis); Robert Cline (*Neptune*); Marilynn Boyd (*Juno*); Frank Keller (*Jupiter*); Lorraine Easton (*Echo*); Helen Virgil (*Diana*); And 1,000 West Coast Beauties (including Jean Arthur).

*The Film:* Based on her screen test, Fox executives heedlessly assigned their novice starlet the female lead in this inconsequential bathing-beauty entertainment. Director Henry Otto shot on location for three days, attempting to get a performance out of the nervous, insecure Jean Arthur before replacing her with Mary Philbin. In the release print, Arthur can still be glimpsed among the extras.

Al St. John and JA in Spring Fever (Fox Film Corp., 1923).

### Spring Fever
(Fox Film Corp.; 1923) Two reels.
Director: Archie Mayo.
Jean Arthur co-starred with former Mack Sennett comic Al St. John (long before he bore the nickname "Fuzzy") in this short "Sunshine" comedy.

### Case Dismissed
(Universal; 1924) One reel.
Director: Slim Summerville.
Jean Arthur teamed with director Summerville and Bobbie Dunn, who played bootleggers, in this comedy short.

## The Powerful Eye

(Universal; 1924) Two reels.

Director: Ernst Laemmle; Scenario: George Morgan; Story: Earle Wayland Bowman.

A Western short, in which Jean Arthur, Pete Morrison and Olin Francis visit a magic show and get into trouble.

## Biff Bang Buddy

(Weiss Brothers Artclass Pictures; 1924) Five reels.

Director: Frank L. Inghram; Story: Reginald C. Barker; Cinematographer: Irving Ries.

*Cast:* Buddy Roosevelt (*Buddy Walters*); Jean Arthur (*Bonnie Norton*); Buck Connors (*Dad Norton*); Robert Fleming (*Shane McCune*); Al Richmond (*Nachez*).

*The Film*: This was the first in a series of low-budget, independently produced Westerns, here casting her opposite Buddy Roosevelt (the newly renamed Kent Sanderson). The cliché-ridden story had hero Roosevelt infiltrating a bandit gang to rescue Arthur.

## Fast and Fearless

(Weiss Brothers Artclass Pictures; 1924) Five reels.

Director: Richard Thorpe. Cinematographer: Irving Ries.

*Cast:* Buffalo Bill Jr. (*Lightning Bill Lewis*); Jean Arthur (*Mary Brown*); William Turner (*Judge Brown*); George Magrill (*Pedro Gomez*); Julian Rivero (*Captain Duerta*); Emily Barrye (*Blanca*); Kewpie King (*Fatty Doolittle*); Steve Clemento (*Gonzales*); Victor Allen (*Sheriff Hawkins*).

*The Film:* In the first of these program Westerns teaming her with Buffalo Bill Jr. (former rodeo champ Jay Wilsey), Arthur's kidnapped by bandit George Magrill and eventually rescued by Bill and the Mexican Rurales.

## Bringin' Home the Bacon

(Weiss Brothers Artclass Pictures; 1924) Five reels.

Director: Richard Thorpe. Producers: W. T. Lackey and Lester F. Scott Jr. Based on the story "Buckin the Big Four" by Christopher B. Booth.

*Cast*: Buffalo Bill Jr. (*Bill Winton*); Jean Arthur (*Nancy Norton*); Bert Lindley (*Joe Breed*); Lafe McKee (*Judge Simpson*); George F. Marion (*Noel Simms*); Wilbur McGaugh (*Jim Allen*); Victor King (*Rastus*); Laura Miskin (*Bertha Abernathy*); Frank Ellis (*The Bandit*).

*The Film:* Released a month after *Fast and Fearless*, this second Buffalo Bill Jr. vehicle casts him as a rancher determined to impress Arthur, but forced to deal with an outlaw gang before their romance can continue.

## Thundering Romance

(Weiss Brothers Artclass Pictures; 1924) Five reels.
Director: Richard Thorpe. Producers: W. T. Lackey and Lester F. Scott Jr.
Story: Ned Nye. Cinematographer: Ray Ries.
*Cast*: Buffalo Bill Jr. (*"Lightning" Bill*); Jean Arthur (*Mary Watkins*); Rene Picot (*Lew Simons*); Harry Todd (*Davey Jones*); Lew Meehan (*Hank Callahan*); J. P. Lockney (*Mark Jennings*); George A. Williams (*The Oil Representative*); Lafe McKee (*Sheriff*).
*The Film:* Arthur's third and final Western with Buffalo Bill Jr. casts her as a rancher who mistakes him for her long-lost brother when Bill seeks refuge from the crooked local Sheriff, following a shoot-out. Director Richard Thorpe, who would graduate to more prestigious pictures at MGM a decade later, has confirmed that Jean Arthur performed all of her own horseback riding in these minor Westerns.

## Travelin' Fast

(Anchor Film Distributors; 1924) Five reels.
*Cast*: Jack Perrin (*Jack Foster*); Jean Arthur (*Betty Conway*); Peggy O'Day (*Ora Perdue*); Lew Meehan (*Red Sampson*); John Pringle (*William Conway*); Horace B. Carpenter (*Sheriff Ted Clark*).
*The Film:* Like Arthur's Artclass releases, this independent Anchor film employed similar plot elements as ranger Jack Perrin brings her father's killers to justice and saves her gold mine. Like most others of its program-Western genre, *Travelin' Fast* clocked in at about an hour.

## Seven Chances

(Metro-Goldwyn-Mayer; 1925) Six reels.
Director: Buster Keaton. Producer: Joseph Schenck. Scenario: Jean Havez, Clyde Bruckman and Joseph Mitchell. Based on the play by Roi Cooper Megrue. Cinematographers: Elgin Lessley and Byron Houck. Art Director: Fred Gabourie. Electrical Effects: Denver Harmon.
*Cast*: Buster Keaton (*James Shannon*); T. Roy Barnes (*His Partner*); Snitz Edwards (*His Lawyer*); Ruth Dwyer (*His Girl*); Frankie Raymond (*Her Mother*); Jules Cowles (*Hired Man*); Erwin Connelly (*Clergyman*); Eugenie Burkette (*Eugenie*); Judy King (*Judy*); Hazel Deane (*Hazel*); Barbara Pierce (*Barbara*); Connie Evans (*Connie*); Pauline Toler (*Pauline*); Jean Arthur (*Receptionist*); Loro Bara, Marion Harlan, Edna Hammon and Rosalind Mooney (*Women*).
*The Film:* In this Buster Keaton production, Jean Arthur appeared with the director-star as a telephone operator. In several scenes, she received no official billing, yet enjoyed one of the larger female roles in the movie. Her best moment involves Keaton's attempt at a proposal, while Arthur reads a book and flashes her wedding ring at him.

Buster Keaton and JA in *Seven Chances*
(Metro-Goldwyn-Mayer, 1925).

### The Drug Store Cowboy
(Independent Pictures; 1925) Five reels.
Director: Park Frame. Story and scenario: Krag Johnson and Burke Jenkins.
*Cast*: Franklyn Farnum (*Marmaduke Grandon*); Robert Walker (*Gentleman Jack*); Jean Arthur (*Jean*); Malcolm Denny (*Wilton*); Ronald Goetz (*Director*); Dick La Reno (*Sheriff*)
*The Film*: Although this minor entry contained Westerns elements, it was more of a comic melodrama, concerning drugstore clerk Farnum's humorous attempts to break into the movies as a cowboy hero. According to Larry Swindell's *The Last Hero: A Biography of Gary Cooper*, that future superstar, then performing in bit parts, appears in *The Drug Store Cowboy* as an extra, holding up the hoof of a horse being shod by Farnum as Arthur watches.

### The Fighting Smile
(Independent Pictures; 1925) Five reels.
Director: Jay Marchant. Producer: Jesse J. Goldburg. Scenario: William A. Burton and Harry J. Brown. Cinematographer: Harry J. Brown.
*Cast*: Bill Cody (*Bud Brant*); Jean Arthur (*Rose Craddock*); with Charles Brinley, George Magrill and Billie Bennett.
*The Film:* Not to be confused with Jean Arthur's former co-star Buffalo Bill Jr., Bill Cody was a Canadian actor who had begun his career in vaudeville and stock productions before graduating to movie stuntman and cowboy star. *The Fighting Smile* casts him as a rancher's son who romances Arthur when not coping with cattle rustlers.

### *Tearin' Loose*

(Weiss Brothers Artclass Pictures; 1925) Five reels.

Director: Richard Thorpe. Producer: Lester F. Scott Jr. Scenario: Frank L. Inghram. Cinematographer: William Marshall.

*Cast*: Wally Wales (*Wally Blake*); Jean Arthur (*Sally Harris*); Charles Whitaker (*Matt Harris*); Alfred Hewston (*Dad Burns*); Polly Vann (*Nora*); Harry Belmour (*Stubb Green*); Bill Ryno (*The Philosopher*); Vester Pegg (*Jim, a Tramp*); Frank Ellis (*The Law*).

*The Film:* For the first of many teamings to come, Jean Arthur appeared opposite Wally Wales, destined to become her most frequent leading man, with five minor-league Westerns. *Tearin' Loose* presents him as a cowboy falsely accused of a crime perpetrated by Arthur's worthless brother (Charles Whitaker). Predictably, Wales eventually clears his name, with the heroine's help.

Reportedly, *Tearin' Loose* was later re-edited into a 10-minute short, produced for home-movie release in the Forties under the title *Gallopin' On.* To confuse matters, the latter was also the name of yet another 1926 Wally Wales Western, one that didn't team him with Jean Arthur.

### *A Man of Nerve*

(Film Booking Offices of America; 1925) Five reels.

Director: Louis Chaudet. Scenario: George Hively. Story: John Harold Hamlin. Cinematographer: Allen Davey.

*Cast:* Bob Custer (*Hackamore Henderson*); Jean Arthur (*Loria Gatlin*); Leon Holmes (*Buddy Simms*); David Dunbar (*Rangey Greer*); Buck Moulton (*Bandit*); Ralph McCullough (*Art Gatlin*).

*The Film*: Bob Custer was another rodeo rider turned Westerns star. In *A Man of Nerve*, heroine Arthur helps the cowboy clear his name after he's unjustly blamed for his employer's killing. Together, they track down the real criminal.

Bob Custer and JA in A Man of Nerve (FBO, 1925).

## The Hurricane Horseman

(Weiss Brothers Artclass Pictures; 1925) Five reels.
Director: Robert Eddy. Scenario: A. E. Serrao and Katherine Fanning.
*Cast:* Wally Wales (*Wally Marden*); Jean Arthur (*June Mathews*); Vester Pegg (*Jim Marden*); Charles Whitaker (*Mike Wesson*); Kewpie King (*Kewpie Cook*); Robert Chandler (*Parson Pettigrew*); Bob Fleming (*Sheriff*).
*The Film:* Working non-stop by now in these low-budget action movies, Arthur was again cast opposite Wally Wales. This time, she's a ranch owner who discovers that her foreman (Charles Whitaker) is guilty of a murder for which Wales' brother (Vester Pegg) was blamed. Bringing the culprit to justice draws Wales and Arthur together.

## Thundering Through

(aka *A Modern Knight*) (Weiss Brothers Artclass Pictures; 1925) Five reels.
Director: Fred Bain. Scenario: Barr Cross
*Cast:* Buddy Roosevelt (*Bud Lawson*); Jean Arthur (*Ruth Burroughs*); Charles Colby (*Blaze Burroughs*); Lew Meehan (*Rufe Gorman*); Frederick Lee (*Aaron Austin*); L. J. O'Connor (*Ezra Hendrix*); Lawrence Underwood (*John Richmond*).
*The Film:* In this reunion teaming of Arthur and Buddy Roosevelt, he plays a cowboy who thwarts a banker's nefarious plan to acquire both his land and that of his sweetheart's father.

## Under Fire

(Davis Distributing Division; 1926) Five reels.
Director: Clifford S. Elfelt. Producer: Albert J. Smith. Adaptation: Frank Howard Clark. Based on the novel by Capt. Charles King.
*Cast:* Bill Patton (*Tom Brennan*); Jean Arthur (*Margaret Cranston*); with Cathleen Calhoun, Norbert Myles, Harry Moody, William Bertram, W. Cassel and H. Renard.
*The Film:* In the busiest year of her career, Jean Arthur enjoyed a temporary respite from Westerns with this independent programmer in which she portrayed the steadfast fiancée of a disgraced Army lieutenant (Bill Patton), who's eventually cleared of unjust charges and reunited with his girl.

## The Roaring Rider

(Weiss Brothers Artclass Pictures; 1926) Five reels.
Director: Richard Thorpe. Screenplay: Reginald C. Barker. Adaptation: Betty Burbridge.
*Cast:* Buffalo Bill Jr., Jean Arthur, Frank Ellis, Hazel Rogers, Charles Whitaker, Bert Lindley.

*The Film:* Standard Western melodrama, with cowboy hero Bill coming to the aid of a ranchers' community terrorized by cattle thieves. Ultimately he defeats the gang and wins pretty local girl Arthur.

### Born to Battle
(Film Booking Offices of America; 1926) Five reels.
Director: Robert DeLacy. Story and Scenario: William E. Wing. Cinematographers: David Smith and Harold Wenstrom.
*Cast:* Tom Tyler (*Dennis Terhune*); Jean Arthur (*Eunice Morgan*); Ray Childs (*Moxley*); Fred Gambold (*Morgan*); Frankie Darro (*Birdie*); Buck Black (*Tuffy*); LeRoy Mason (*Daley*); Ethan Laidlaw (*Trube*).
*The Film*: Her second picture for release by FBO cast Arthur opposite popular cowboy star Tom Tyler, as a ranch foreman who falls for the boss's daughter.

### The Fighting Cheat
(Weiss Brothers Artclass Pictures; 1926) Five reels.
Director: Richard Thorpe. Scenario: Betty Burbridge.
*Cast:* Wally Wales (*Wally Kenyon*); Jean Arthur (*Ruth Wells*); Ted Rackerby (*Lafe Wells*); Fanny Midgley (*Mrs. Wells*); Charles Whitaker (*Jud Nolan*); V. L. Banes (*Doctor*); Al Taylor (*Cook*).
The Film: In a variation on the standard storyline, Arthur played the sister of a bandit (Ted Rackerby) who's abducted, but later rescued by hero Wally Wales.

### Eight-Cylinder Bull
(Fox Film Corp.; 1926) Two reels.
Directors: Alfred Davis, Max Gold and Jack Leys. Scenario: Jack Leys. Story: Walter Ruben and Sydney Lanfield
Jean Arthur teamed with Harold Austin and Ralph Sipperly in this slapstick farce about a used-car salesman. With Scott Seaton.

### The Mad Racer
(Fox Film Corp.; 1926) Two reels.
Director: Ben Stoloff. Scenario: Mark Sandrich. Based on the short story "Van Bibber at the Races" by Richard Harding Davis.
Jean Arthur teamed with Earle Foxe and Florence Gilbert in this episode in Fox's Van Bibber comedy series. The cast included Frank Beal, Lynn Cowan, Lawford Davies, Frank Cooley, Patrick Rooney, Edna Marian and Jere Austin.

### Riding Rivals

(Weiss Brothers Artclass Pictures; 1926) Five reels.
Director: Richard Thorpe. Screenplay: Betty Burbridge.
*Cast:* Wally Wales, Jean Arthur, Charles Colby, Frank Ellis, Fanny Midgely, Charles Whitaker, William H. Turner, Lafe McKee.
*The Film*: In her fifth minor Western opposite Wally Wales, Jean Arthur worked for the seventh time with director Richard Thorpe. While mastering the mechanics of moviemaking, she was scarcely learning anything about the art of acting.

### Double Daring

(Weiss Brothers Artclass Pictures; 1926) Five reels.
Director: Richard Thorpe. Story: Betty Burbridge. Continuity: Frank L. Inghram.
*Cast*: Wally Wales (*Wally Meeker*); J. P. Lockney (*Banker Wells*); Jean Arthur (*Marie Wells*); Hank Bell (*Lee Falcon*); Charles Whitaker (*Blackie Gorman*); Toby Wing (*Nan*); H. E. Hendrix (*The Law*).
*The Film:* On what must have seemed like a punishing treadmill, Arthur collaborated yet again with director Richard Thorpe and co-star Wally Wales on another routine B-Western. It was released a mere six weeks after its predecessor, *Riding Rivals*, in the late spring of 1926. The film is noteworthy for an early appearance of future Thirties platinum-blonde starlet Toby Wing, here cast as an orphaned child.

### Lightning Bill

(Goodwill Pictures; 1926) Five reels.
Director: Louis Chaudet.
*Cast:* Bill Bailey (*William W. Williams*); Jean Arthur (*Marie Denton*); Edward Heim (*John R. Denton*); Jack Henderson (*Edward G. Hookem*); Charles Meakin (*Daniel Carson*); Tom Shirley (*Lionel Jay Murphy*).
The Film: In her one-and-only acting stint for the independent Goodwill Pictures, Jean Arthur was the love interest of a two-fisted rancher (Bill Bailey), who loses his nerve in the wake of a fall. Nearly swindled out of oil rich land, he regains his senses in time to foil the crooks and win the girl.

### Twisted Triggers

(Associated Exhibitors; 1926) Five reels.
Director: Richard Thorpe. Producer: Lester F. Scott Jr. Story: Tommy Gray. Continuity: Betty Burbridge. Cinematographer: Ray Ries.
*Cast:* Wally Wales (*Wally Weston*); Jean Arthur (*Ruth Regan*); Al Richmond (*Norris*); Art Winkler (*"Angel-Face"*); J. P. Lockney (*Hiram*

*Weston*); William Bertram (*Jim Regan*); Harry Belmour (*Cook*); Lawrence Underwood (*Sheriff*).

*The Film:* In the last of Jean Arthur's action programmers with Wally Wales and director Richard Thorpe, our cowboy hero tracks down the man who killed her father. *Twisted Triggers* would also mark Arthur's final appearance in an independent B-Western. In the words of *Photoplay*'s reviewer: "There is no reason why you should waste a perfectly good hour on this nonsense."

### The Cowboy Cop

(Film Booking Offices of America; 1926) Five reels.

Director: Robert DeLacy. Producer: Joseph P. Kennedy. Story: Frank Richardson Pierce. Continuity: F. A. E. Pine. Cinematographer: John Leezer. Assistant Director: John Burch.

*Cast:* Tom Tyler (*Jerry McGill*); Jean Arthur (*Virginia Selby*); Irvin Renard (*Count Mirski*); Frankie Darro (*Frankie*); Pat Harmon (*Dago Jack, First Crook*); Earl Haley (*Second Crook*); Beans (*Himself, a dog*).

*The Film:* Notwithstanding its title, *The Cowboy Cop* isn't a Western, despite some peripheral generic elements. It's set in contemporary Los Angeles, where Arizona cow puncher Tom Tyler becomes a mounted policeman and wins Arthur's heart when he saves her from big-city jewel thieves.

JA, Frankie Darro and Tom Tyler in The Cowboy Cop (FBO, 1926).

### The College Boob

(Film Booking Offices of America; 1926) Six reels.

Director: Harry Garson. Producer: Joseph P. Kennedy. Story: Jack Casey. Cinematographer: James Brown.

*Cast:* Lefty Flynn (*Aloysius Appleby*); Jean Arthur (*Angela Boothby*); Jimmy Anderson (*Horatio Winston Jr.*); Bob Bradbury Jr. (*Shorty Buzelle*); Cecil Ogden (*Smacky McNeil*); Dorothea Wolbert (*Aunt Polly*); William Malan (*Uncle Lish*); Raymond Turner (*Whitewinds Washington*).
*The Film:* In a complete departure from her surfeit of Western heroines, Jean Arthur plays a coed who's instrumental in helping hapless hero Lefty Flynn score in the big football game. The movie was obviously designed to cash in on the mid-Twenties interest in collegiate subject matter in the wake of Harold Lloyd's 1925 hit comedy *The Freshman*.

### *The Block Signal*
(Lumas Film Corp., 1926) Six reels.
Director: Frank O'Connor. Producer: Sam Sax. Screenplay: Frank O'Connor. Continuity: Edward J. Meagher. Story: F. Oakley Crawford. Cinematographer: Ray June.
*Cast:* Ralph Lewis (*"Jovial Joe" Ryan*); Jean Arthur (*Grace Ryan*); Hugh Allan (*Jack Milford*); George Cheeseboro (*Bert Steele*); Sidney Franklin (*"Roadhouse" Rosen*); Leon Holmes (*"Unhandy" Andy*); Jim Brennan (*"Missouri" Royer*).
*The Film:* Jean Arthur was again the heroine of an independent release, this time as a locomotive engineer's daughter in a romantic railroad melodrama. In the first nine months of 1926, the moviegoing public had been offered no less than 13 minor-league pictures featuring Jean Arthur!

JA and Hugh Allen in The Block Signal
(Gotham Productions/Lumas Film Corp., 1926).

### Husband Hunters

(Tiffany Productions; 1927) Six reels.

Director: John G. Adolfi. Producer: M. H. Hoffman. Story: Douglas Bronston. Adaptation: Esther Shulkin. Cinematographers: Joseph A. Dubray and Steve Norton. Editor: Harold Young. Art Director: Edwin B. Willis.

*Cast:* Mae Busch (*Marie Devere*); Charles Delaney (*Bob Garrett*); Jean Arthur (*Letty Crane*); Walter Hiers (*Sylvester Jones*); Duane Thompson (*Helen Gray*); Mildred Harris (*Cynthia Kane*); Robert Cain (*Bartley Mortimer*); Jimmy Harrison (*Jimmy Wallace*); Nigel Barrie (*Rex Holden*); James Mack (*Mr. Casey*); Marcin Asher (*Mr. Cohen*); Alfred Fisher (*Archibald Springer*).

Mae Busch, JA and Mildred Harris in
Husband Hunters
(Tiffany Productions, 1927).

The Film: The first of her two 1927 pictures for Tiffany Productions, *Husband Hunters* allotted Jean Arthur third billing as a small-town innocent who relocates to the big city in hopes of becoming a chorus girl. This sophisticated comedy melodrama had her nearly led astray by millionaire villain Robert Cain, before winding up with good guy Charles Delaney.

In the press, things were beginning to look up. *Exhibitor's Daily* remarked, "It serves to bring Jean Arthur into the spotlight." And *Photoplay* dubbed *Husband Hunters* "Trivial but fairly amusing."

### Hello! Lafayette!

(aka: *Lafayette, Where Are We?*) (Fox Film Corp.; 1927) Two reels.

Directors: Max Gold and Al Davis. Story: Gene Ford and Henry Johnson.

*The Film:* An apparent delayed release from her last days at Fox, this short "Imperial" comedy cast her as the feminine lead opposite Ernie Shields and Harry Woods.

### The Broken Gate

(Tiffany Productions; 1927) Six reels.

Director: James C. McKay. Scenario and Continuity: John Francis Natteford. Based on the novel by Emerson Hough. Cinematographers: Joseph A. Dubray and Stephen Norton. Editors: Harold Young and Merrill White. Art Direction: Edwin B. Willis.

*Cast:* Dorothy Phillips (*Aurora Lane*); William Collier Jr. (*Don Lane*); Jean Arthur (*Ruth Hale*); Phillips Smalley (*Judge Lucius Henderson*); Florence Turner (*Miss Julia*); Gibson Gowland (*Ephraim Adamson*); Charles A. Post (*Johnny Adamson*); Caroline "Spike" Rankin (*Ms. Ephraim Adamson*); Vera Lewis (*Invalid*); Jack McDonald (*Sheriff Dan Cummins*); Charles Thurston (*Constable Joe Tarbush*); Adele Watson (*Gossip*).

*The Film:* Adapted from Emerson Hough's novel about the after-effects of illegitimacy on a small American town, this drama starred Dorothy Phillips as a woman treated with local contempt for having had a child out of wedlock 20 years earlier. At college, her son (William "Buster" Collier Jr.) falls for a co-ed (Jean Arthur), who's the ward of a respected judge (Phillips Smalley), who happens to be the boy's birth-father. Predictable complications ensue. While complimenting the cast, *Variety*'s critic concluded, "It will have to be a pretty dumb fan clientele that will take the picture seriously."

### Bigger and Better Blondes

(Pathé; 1927) Two reels.
Director: James Parrott. Producer: Hal Roach.
Cast: Charley Chase, Mario Carillo, Jean Arthur, Gale Henry, Frank Brownlee.

*The Film:* For her final appearance in a short, Arthur worked at the prestigious Hal Roach studios, as leading lady to the popular comedian Charley Chase. Here, he's a delivery boy with a package for Arthur, on whom he develops a crush, with humorous results.

### Horse Shoes

(Pathé Exchange; 1927) Six reels.
Director: Clyde Bruckman. Producer: A. MacArthur. Scenario and Story: Monty Banks and Charles Horan. Cinematographer: James Diamond.

*Cast:* Monty Banks (*Monty Milde*); Ernie Wood (*Henry Baker Jr.*); Henry Barrows (*Henry Baker Sr.*); John Elliott (*William Baker*); Jean Arthur (*His Daughter*); Arthur Thalasso (*Conductor*); George French (*Mayor*); Bert Apling (*O'Toole*); Agostino Borgato (*Judge*).

*The Film:* The first of her two pictures produced by knockabout comedian Monty Banks for his own company cast Arthur as a young woman who's aided by Banks in contesting a will. An amusing early sequence focuses on their embarrassment during a train journey when they're mistaken for newlyweds.

William Baker, Monty Banks and JA in Horse Shoes
(Pathé, 1927).

### The Poor Nut

(First National; 1927) Seven reels.

Director: Richard Wallace. Producer: Jess Smith. Screenplay and continuity: Paul Schofield. Based on the Play by J. C. Nugent and Elliott Nugent. Cinematographer: David Kesson.

*Cast:* Jack Mulhall (*John Miller*); Charlie Murray (*"Doc"*); Jean Arthur (*Margie*); Jane Winton (*Julia*); Glenn Tryon (*"Magpie" Welch*); Cornelius Keefe (*Wallie Pierce*); Maurice Ryan (*"Hub" Smith*); Henry Vibart (*Professor Demming*); Bruce Gordon (*Coach Jackson*); William Courtwright (*Colonel Small*).

*The Film*: Jean Arthur and Jane Winton played co-eds competing for the affections of track star Jack Mulhall in this college comedy. The movie at least attracted some press attention to Arthur: for the first time, the *New York Times* actually made mention of her, noting "the appeal of Jean Arthur." *Variety*, on the other hand, took space to criticize both leading ladies as "flat specimens," lacking in both screen presence and photogenic appeal.

### The Masked Menace

(Pathé; 1927) A 10-chapter serial.

Director: Arch Heath. Screenplay: Paul Fairfax Fuller. Based on the story "Still Face" by Clarence Budington Kelland. Chapter titles: (1) "Against Odds," (2) "An Unknown Assassin," (3) "The Enemy Strikes," (4) "A Half-Wit's Fury," (5) "An Attack at Midnight," (6) "Checkmate," (7) "By Hook or Crook," (8) "Still Face Shows His Hand," (9) "The Last Stand," (10) "The Menace Unmasked."

*Cast:* Larry Kent, Jean Arthur, Tom Holding, Laura Alberta, John F. Hamilton, Gus DeWeil, Agnes Dome.

*The Film:* In her only foray into the serial genre, Jean Arthur played the menaced heroine to Larry Kent's hero. An adaptation of Clarence Budington Kelland's *Saturday Evening Post* story "Still Face" (the villain's name), this chapter-play appears no longer to exist. A clue to its quality lies in Kalton Lahue's book *Bound and Gagged*, which states that director Arch Heath's four productions from this era were "among the poorest serials ever released by Pathé."

Larry Kent, Thomas Holding and JA in The Masked Menace
(Pathé, 1927).

### Flying Luck

(Pathé Exchange; 1927) Seven reels.

Director: Herman C. Raymaker. Scenario: Charles Horan and Matt Taylor. Story: Charles Horan and Monty Banks. Cinematographers: James Diamond and Stanley Norsley. Editor: William Holmes. Assistant Directors: Ray McDevitt and Arthur Varney.

*Cast:* Monty Banks (*The Boy*); Jean Arthur (*The Girl*); J. W. Johnston (*The Colonel*); Kewpie Morgan (*The Sergeant*); Eddie Chandler (*The Corporal*); Silver Harr (*The Orderly*).

*The Film*: The last of Arthur's eight pictures released in 1927, *Flying Luck* was one of several aviation-themed features designed to cash in on public interest generated by Lindbergh's groundbreaking flight from New York to Paris in May of that year. In this Monty Banks comedy, he's an amateur flyer who joins the Army and becomes an air hero. Arthur played the colonel's vivacious daughter, impressed by Banks' exploits. *Variety*'s critic was less impressed, assessing this one as "merely a two-reeler padded with extra falls and ineffective mugging as filler for the additional running time."

## Wallflowers
(Film Booking Offices of America; 1928) Seven reels.
Director: Leo Meehan. Scenario: Dorothy Yost. Based on the novel by Temple Bailey. Cinematographer: Allen Siegler. Editor: Edward Schroeder. Assistant Director: Charles Kerr.
*Cast:* Hugh Trevor (*Rufus*); Mabel Julienne Scott (*Sherry*); Charles Stevenson (*Mr. Fish*); Jean Arthur (*Sandra*); Lola Todd (*Theodora*); Tempe Pigott (*Mrs. Claybourne*); Crauford Kent (*Maulsby*); Reginald Simpson (*Markham*).
*The Film:* Arthur played a sweet young thing from Virginia who leaves home with her sister (Lola Todd), bent on impressing Washington society, and ultimately finding romance with Hugh Trevor. *Variety* found little to praise in the performances, and called the picture "tiresome."

## Warming Up
(Paramount; 1928) Eight reels.
Director: Fred Newmeyer. Produced by Adolph Zukor and Jesse L. Lasky. Adaptation and Screenplay: Ray Harris. Story: Sam Mintz. Cinematographer: Edward Cronjager. Titles: George Marion Jr. Editor: Otto Levering. Song "Out of the Dawn" by Walter Donaldson. Musical Score and Sound Effects by Movietone.
*Cast:* Richard Dix (*Bert Tulliver*); Jean Arthur (*Mary Post*); Claude King (*Mr. Post*); Philo McCullough (*McRae*); Billy Kent Schaefer (*Edsel*); Roscoe Karns (*Hippo*); James Dugan (*Brill*); Mike Donlin (*Veteran*); Mike Ready, Chet Thomas, Joe Pirrone, Wally Hood, Bob Murray and Truck Hannah (*Themselves*); Wade Boteler (*Doyle*).
*The Film:* By mid-July of 1928, when *Warming Up* was released, Hollywood's gradual transition from silent pictures to talkies resulted in many pictures, originally shot silent, having the addition of sound effects, talking sequences and musical sound tracks prior to release. This was Paramount's initial experiment with sound. And yet, since many cinemas were not yet sufficiently equipped, *Warming Up* was released in both sound and silent versions. However, synchronization remained a problem in this instance, and the *New York Times* critic noted that the smack of baseball against bat was heard some seconds before the batter's windup.
Jean Arthur played a ball-club owner's daughter who helps a small town's star pitcher (Richard Dix) graduate into the big leagues. Complications involve his bitter rivalry with teammate Philo McCullough, both on the diamond and for the affections of Arthur.

*Variety* found little praise for *Warming Up*: "Without the sound effects . . . the picture is one of the worst duds ever to come out of the Hollywood factory. While the sound record doesn't synchronize . . . it lifts the thing unbelievably. The excitement of the crowd is in some measures transferred to the audience, making the ridiculous story almost plausible at the end, and helping the World's Series sequence build up to a dramatic climax."

Unfortunately, for this her first picture for Paramount, the actress was cited for her "beauty and personality," but credited as "June" Arthur.

### Brotherly Love

(Metro-Goldwyn-Mayer; 1928) Seven reels.
Director: Charles F. Reisner. Scenario: Earl Baldwin and Lew Lipton. Based on the story "Big-Hearted Jim" by Patterson Margoni. Cinematographer: Henry Sharp. Editor: George Hively. Art Director: Cedric Gibbons. Wardrobe: Henrietta Frazer. Talking Sequences and Sound Effects by Movietone.
*Cast:* Karl Dane (*Oscar*); George K. Arthur (*Jerry*); Jean Arthur (*Mary*); Richard Carlyle (*Warden Brown*); Edward Connelly (*Coggswell*); Marcia Harris (*Mrs. Coggswell*).
*The Film:* Instead of utilizing their new contract player in a Paramount picture, the studio loaned Arthur to MGM for this satire on prison reform with the comedy team of Karl Dane and George K. Arthur. Here she's the warden's pretty daughter, admired by both dumb guard Dane and refined inmate Arthur. At the movie's climax, the latter scores a touchdown in the prison football game and wins the heroine's love. Like its predecessor, *Brotherly Love* was released in both sound and silent versions, although it was only a partial-talkie.

### Sins of the Fathers

(Paramount; 1928) Ten reels.
Director: Ludwig Berger. Adaptation: E. Lloyd Sheldon. Story: Norman Burnstine. Titles: Julian Johnson. Cinematographer: Victor Milner. Editor: Frances Marsh. Musical Score: Hugo Riesenfeld. Sound Effects and Musical Score by Movietone.
*Cast:* Emil Jannings (*Wilhelm Spengler*); Ruth Chatterton (*Gretta*); Barry Norton (*Tom Spengler*); Jean Arthur (*Mary Spengler*); Jack Luden (*Otto*); ZaSu Pitts (*Mother Spengler*); Matthew Betz (*Gus the Bartender*); Harry Cording (*The Highjacker*); Arthur Housman (*The Count*); Frank Reicher (*The Eye Specialist*); Douglas Haig (*Tom as a Boy*); Dawn O'Day (*Mary as a Girl*).
*The Film:* Tailored for Paramount's distinguished German character star Emil Jannings, this melodrama about alcoholism cast him as a married

restaurant owner led astray by a woman (Ruth Chatterton) who gets him into the bootlegging business. In the process, his wife (ZaSu Pitts) dies of a broken heart, his son (Barry Norton) goes blind from drinking his father's bad liquor, and Jannings goes to jail. Jean Arthur had the unrewarding supporting role of his daughter, played as a child in the film's early scenes by young Dawn O'Day. The latter would enjoy her own minor stardom in the mid-Thirties, after changing her name to Anne Shirley. *Sins of the Fathers* was shown in both sound and silent versions.

JA models a stylish evening frock
(Paramount Pictures, 1928).

## The Canary Murder Case

(Paramount; 1929) Seven reels.
Directors: Malcolm St. Clair and (uncredited) Frank Tuttle. Associate Producer: Louis D. Lighton. Story and Dialogue by S. S. Van Dine, based on his novel. Adaptation: Albert Shelby LeVino. Screenplay: Florence Ryerson. Titles (Silent Version): Herman J. Mankiewicz. Cinematographer: Harry Fischbeck. Editor: William Shea.
*Cast:* William Powell (*Philo Vance*); Jean Arthur (*Alice LaFosse*); James Hall (*Jimmy Spotswoode*); Louise Brooks (*Margaret "The Canary" O Dell*); Charles Lane (*Charles Spotswoode*); Lawrence Grant (*John Cleaver*); Gustav von Seyffertitz (*Dr. Ambrose Lindquist*); E. H. Calvert (*District Attorney Markham*); Eugene Pallette (*Sergeant Heath*); Ned Sparks (*Tony Skeel*); Louis John Bartel (*Louis Mannix*); Oscar Smith (*Hallboy*).
*The Film*: In this initial filming of an S. S. Van Dine murder mystery, William Powell enjoyed his first of several assignments as the urbane

literary detective Philo Vance. It's all about the murder of a blackmailing night-club performer known as "The Canary" (Louise Brooks). Jean Arthur's role, extraneous to the mystery plot, is simply the love interest for prime suspect James Hall.

Produced as a silent, the movie was partially re-shot (by uncredited director Frank Tuttle) as a full-fledged talkie, although the original version remained available to theatres not yet converted to sound. And, while Louise Brooks' voice was dubbed (none too successfully) by Margaret Livingston), Jean Arthur was heard, for the first time on screen, speaking in her own distinctive voice. The results were negligible and, reportedly, not a little embarrassing to the actress.

### Stairs of Sand
(Paramount; 1929) Six reels.
Director: Otto Brower. Adaptation: Agnes Brand Leahy, Sam Mintz and J. Walter Ruben. Based on the novel by Zane Grey. Titles: Ben Grauman Kohn. Cinematographer: Rex Wimpy. Editor: Frances Marsh.
*Cast:* Wallace Beery (*Guerd Larey*); Jean Arthur (*Ruth Hutt*); Phillips Holmes (*Adam Wansfell*); Fred Kohler (*Boss Stone*); Chester Conklin (*Tim*); Guy Oliver (*Sheriff Collishaw*); Lillian Worth (*Babe*); Frank Rice (*Stage Driver*); Clarence L. Sherwood (*Waiter*).
*The Film*: One of a series of silent Westerns based on the popular novels of Zane Grey, *Stairs of Sand* was so cheaply and quickly made that Paramount didn't even bother to add sound elements to the finished product before release in June of 1929. Actually, its production marked the completion of troublesome character star Wallace Beery's studio contract, and the shoot was apparently not a happy one. He played a sympathetic outlaw whose ultimate self-sacrifice anticipates a happy future for the story's young romantic leads, Jean Arthur and Phillips Holmes. *Variety* called the picture a "mild Western thriller that might get by in the remote grinds on a double bill, mainly on the strength of the featured players."

### The Mysterious Dr. Fu Manchu
(Paramount; 1929) 81 minutes.
Director: Rowland V. Lee. Screenplay and dialogue: Florence Ryerson, Lloyd Corrigan and George Marion Jr. Based on the novel *The Insidious Dr. Fu Manchu* by Sax Rohmer. Cinematographer: Harry Fischbeck. Editor (Sound Version): George Nichols Jr. Editor (Silent Version): Bronson Howard. Sound Engineer: Eugene Merritt.
*Cast:* Warner Oland (*Dr. Fu Manchu*); Neil Hamilton (*Dr. Jack Petrie*); Jean Arthur (*Lia Eltham*); O. P. Heggie (*Nayland Smith*); William Austin (*Sylvester Wadsworth*); Claude King (*Sir John Petrie*); Charles Stevenson

(*General Petrie*); Evelyn Selbie (*Fai Lo*); Noble Johnson (*Li Po*); Charles Giblyn (*Weymouth*); Donald MacKenzie (*Trent*); Lawford Davidson (*Clarkson*); Laska Winter (*Fu Mela*); Charles Stevens (*Singh*); Chappel Dossett (*Reverend Mr. Eltham*); Tully Marshall (*Ambassador*).

*The Film*: This all-talking picture (also released in a silent version) afforded Jean Arthur a bit more range than her previous Paramount assignments, which may account for her improved acting. Here, she's the adopted daughter of the nefarious Oriental Dr. Fu, who's bent on wiping out a number of British officers he believes caused his family's demise. His plot involves hypnotizing Arthur to carry out his revenge plans, until she's rescued by romantic lead Neil Hamilton and police inspector O. P. Heggie. In the *New York Times'* assessment, "The whole, if you like melodrama, is very good."

Warner Oland and JA in The Mysterious Dr. Fu Manchu
(Paramount Pictures, 1929).

## The Greene Murder Case

(Paramount; 1929) 71 minutes.

Director: Frank Tuttle. Screenplay: Louise Long and Bartlett Cormack. Based on the novel by S. S. Van Dine. Titles (Silent Version): Richard H. Digges Jr. Cinematographer: Henry Gerard.

*Cast*: William Powell (*Philo Vance*); Florence Eldridge (*Sibella Greene*); Ullrich Haupt (*Dr. Von Blon*); Jean Arthur (*Ada Greene*); Eugene Pallette (*Sergeant Heath*); E. H. Calvert (*District Attorney Markham*); Gertrude Norman (*Mrs. Tobias Greene*); Lowell Drew (*Chester Greene*); Morgan Farley (*Rex Greene*); Brandon Hurst (*Sproot*); Augusta Burmeister (*Mrs. Mannheim*); Marcia Harris (*Hemming*); Mildred Golden (*Barton*); Mrs. Wilfred Buckland (*Mrs. Greene's Nurse*); Helena Phillips (*Miss O'Brien*);

Shep Camp (*Medical Examiner*); Charles E. Evans (*Lawyer Canon*); Harry Strong (*Cop*).

*The Film*: Like *The Canary Murder Case*, this second Philo Vance mystery was released in both sound and silent versions. Again cast as Vance, William Powell here sets out to investigate a series of New York killings in a gloomy East River mansion where members of the unhappy, neurotic Greene family, forced to cohabit by the terms of a will, are being murdered one by one. Although believable as the sweet, innocent Ada Greene, Jean Arthur turns out to be a mentally unbalanced killer. In the movie's climax, she tries to push sister Florence Eldridge from the mansion's roof, but instead falls to her own death in the river below.

A better film than its S. S. Van Dine predecessor in every department, *The Greene Murder Case* offered Arthur a more challenging character that director Frank Tuttle helped her bring off to the extent that *Photoplay* magazine called her performance "distinguished."

Florence Eldridge and JA in The Greene Murder Case
(Paramount Pictures, 1929).

### *The Saturday Night Kid*

(Paramount; 1929) 65 minutes.

Director: A. Edward Sutherland. Screenplay: Ethel Doherty. Dialogue: Lloyd Corrigan and Edward Paramore Jr. Based on the play *Love 'em and Leave 'em* by George Abbott and John V. A. Weaver. Cinematographer: Harry Fischbeck. Editor: Jane Loring.

*Cast*: Clara Bow (*Mayme Barry*); James Hall (*William Taylor*); Jean Arthur (*Janie Barry*); Charles Sellon (*Lem Woodruff*); Ethel Wales (*Ma Woodruff*); Edna May Oliver (*Miss Streeter*); Hyman Meyer (*Ginsberg*); Eddie Dunn

(*Jim*); Frank Ross (*Ken*); Leone Lane (*Pearl*); Jean Harlow (*Hazel*); Getty Bird (*Rich Ginsberg*); Alice Adair (*Girl*); Irving Bacon (*McGonigle*); Mary Gordon (*Reducing Customer*); Ernie S. Adams (*Gambler*); Bess Flowers (*Another Customer*).

*The Film*: Based on *Love 'em and Leave 'em*, this was the second screen version of the George Abbott-John V.A. Weaver play, which Paramount had made but three years earlier in a silent film starring Evelyn Brent, Lawrence Grey and Louise Brooks in the roles now given voice by Clara Bow, James Hall and Jean Arthur. As the self-centered, irresponsible sister of sensible, hard-working Bow, Arthur has the more colorful part. They're both salesgirls in a department store, with Arthur not only preempting Bow's beau (Hall), but also gambling away some borrowed funds, for which Bow takes the blame. By the movie's end, Hall is reunited with his original girl.

As Janie Barry in The Saturday Night Kid
(Paramount Pictures, 1929).

Jean Arthur's role here allowed her an enjoyable display of character, and her performance attracted some praiseworthy critical notice. The *New York Times* found hers "a thoroughly believable and natural portrayal," concluding "Jean Arthur almost manages major honors." In what *Variety* termed "the whinnying role of younger sister," they thought that Arthur "fits it in voice and appearance." In fact, so effective is her whiny, manipulative characterization that she tends to become quite annoying before her justifiable come-uppance in the movie's final scenes. Future Thirties sex symbol Jean Harlow makes an early appearance here as a salesgirl colleague of Bow and Arthur, but her scenes are brief and director

Sutherland apparently saw little promise in her screen presence, for the camera does her no favors, and one has to look fast to notice her.
Paramount issued *The Saturday Night Kid* in both sound and silent versions.

### Half Way to Heaven

(Paramount; 1929) 66 minutes.
Director: George Abbott. Adaptation: George Abbott. Based on the novel *Here Comes the Bandwagon* by Henry Leyford Gates. Titles (Silent Version): Gerald Geraghty. Cinematographers: Alfred Gilks and Charles Lang. Editor: William Shea. Recording Engineer: Earl Hayman.
*Cast:* Charles "Buddy" Rogers (*Ned Lee*); Jean Arthur (*Greta Nelson*); Paul Lukas (*Nick Polgi*); Helen Ware (*Madame Elsie*); Oscar Apfel (*The Manager*); Edna West (*Mrs. Lee*); Irving Bacon (*Slim*); Nestor Aber (*Eric*); Al Hill (*Blackie*); Lucille Williams (*Doris*); Richard K. French (*Klein*); Freddy Anderson (*Tony*); Ford West (*Stationmaster*); Guy Oliver (*Farmer*).
*The Film*: An above-average drama of circus life, *Half Way to Heaven* teamed Arthur with Charles "Buddy" Rogers as tightrope partners in a circus, where jealous colleague Paul Lukas creates a menacing love triangle. Already responsible for the death of another aerialist who caught Arthur's fancy, he provides an ever-threatening presence to Rogers' safety in performance. After Rogers thwarts Lukas's plan to kill him, as well, the latter is fired from the circus, cementing the lovers' relationship.

Charles "Buddy" Rogers and JA in Half Way to Heaven
(Paramount Pictures, 1929).

Although George Abbott's direction drew the picture's most complimentary attention, Arthur was termed "appealing" by the *New York Times*' Mordaunt

Hall, who cited her "easy way of talking and grace of manner." *Variety*'s critic called her a "good-looking girl" who "may be going somewhere."

### Street of Chance

(Paramount; 1930) 76 minutes.

Director: John Cromwell. Scenario: Howard Estabrook. Story and Dialogue: Oliver H. P. Garrett. Titles (Silent Version): Gerald Geraghty. Dialogue: Lenore J. Coffee. Cinematographer: Charles Lang. Editor: Otto Levering. Sound: Harry D. Mills.

*Cast:* William Powell (*"Natural Davis"/J. B. Marsden*); Kay Francis (*Alma Marsden*); Regis Toomey (*Babe Marsden*); Jean Arthur (*Judith Marsden*); Stanley Fields (*Dorgan*); Brooks Benedict (*Al Mastick*); Betty Francisco (*Mrs. Mastick*); John Risso (*Tony*); Joan Standing (*Miss Abrams*); Maurice Black (*Nick*); Irving Bacon (*Harry*); John Cromwell (*Imbrie*).

*The Film:* One of Paramount's more important releases of 1930, *Street of Chance* was a first-rate thriller based on the Arnold Rothstein murder case. William Powell played the (thinly disguised) New York City gambler, with Kay Francis as the wife who's ready to walk out on their marriage, because of his criminal associations. Jean Arthur had an unimportant supporting role as the bride, who becomes the widow, of Powell's gambling younger brother, Regis Toomey.

Of little importance to Arthur's career, *Street of Chance* attracted favorable attention and enjoyed box-office success, winning an Academy Award nomination for Howard Estabrook's screenplay. Once again, the film was made available in sound and silent versions. Paramount remade it in 1937 as *Her Husband Lies*, with Ricardo Cortez and Gail Patrick.

William Powell and JA in Street of Chance
(Paramount Pictures, 1930).

### *Young Eagles*

(Paramount; 1930) 72 minutes.

Director: William A. Wellman. Scenario: Grover Jones and William Slavens McNutt. Based on the stories "The One Who Was Clever" and "Sky-High" by Elliott White Springs. Cinematographer: Archie J. Stout. Editor: Allyson Shaffer. Assistant Director: Charles Barton. Recording Engineer: Eugene Merritt. Songs: "Love, Here Is My Heart" by Ross Adrian and Leo Silesu; "The Sunrise and You" by Arthur A. Penn.

*Cast:* Charles Rogers (*Lt. Gene Banks*); Jean Arthur (*Mary Gordon*); Paul Lukas (*Von Koch*); Stuart Erwin (*Lt. Pudge Higgins*); Virginia Bruce (*Florence Welford*); Gordon De Main (*Major Lewis*); James Finlayson (*Scotty*); Frank Ross (*Lt. Graham*); Jack Luden (*Lt. Barker*); Freeman Wood (*Lt. Mason*); George Irving (*Col. Wilder*); Stanley Blystone (Capt. Deming).

*The Film*: Coming from William A. Wellman, the Oscar-winning director of 1927's *Wings*, this World War I melodrama understandably won acclaim for its aerial scenes. But its unintentionally amusing script had a none-too-convincing Jean Arthur as an American spy who poses as a German spy and finds romance with Charles Rogers during his leave in Paris.

In what now sounds like radical miscasting, *Variety* described Arthur as being "seductively squeezed into a dress that's conspicuous for snugness" while impersonating "America's most gifted woman spy." No wonder that the *New York Times* reported, "Jean Arthur seems to be somewhat afraid of the character she plays."

Again, Paramount released sound and silent versions.

Charles Rogers, JA, Paul Lukas and Virginia Bruce in Young Eagles
(Paramount Pictures, 1930).

## *Paramount on Parade*

(Paramount: 1930) 102 minutes.

Directors: Dorothy Arzner, Otto Brower, Edmund Goulding, Victor Heerman, Edwin H. Knopf, Rowland V. Lee, Ernst Lubitsch, Lothar Mendes, Victor Shertzinger, A. Edward Sutherland and Frank Tuttle. Producer: Albert S. Kaufman. Production Supervisor: Elsie Janis. Dance Ensembles: David Bennett. Cinematographers: Harry Fischbeck and Victor Milner. Art Director: John Wenger.

*Cast:* (in alphabetical order): Iris Adrian, Richard Arlen, Jean Arthur, Mischa Auer, William Austin, George Bancroft, Clara Bow, Evelyn Brent, Mary Brian, Clive Brook, Virginia Bruce, Nancy Carroll, Ruth Chatterton, Maurice Chevalier, Gary Cooper, Cecil Cunningham, Leon Errol, Stuart Erwin, Stanley Fields, Henry Fink, Kay Francis, Skeets Gallagher, Harry Green, Mitzi Green, James Hall, Phillips Holmes, Helen Kane, Dennis King, Abe Lyman and His Band, Fredric March, Nino Martini, Mitzi Mayfair, the Marion Morgan Dancers, David Newell, Jack Oakie, Warner Oland, Zelma O'Neal, Eugene Pallette, Joan Peers, Jack Pennick, William Powell, Charles "Buddy" Rogers, Lillian Roth, Rolfe Sedan, Stanley Smith and Fay Wray.

*The Film:* Cashing in on the then-current trend to produce all-star musical revues, this was Paramount's well-received answer to Fox's *Happy Days*, MGM's *Hollywood Revue of 1929* and Warner Bros.' *Show of Shows*.

Unlike many of her Paramount colleagues, Jean Arthur appeared twice in this extravaganza: in a hospital skit, she's a nurse opposite comedian Leon Errol; and in her first experience with early, two-strip Technicolor, Arthur shares the Old South musical number "Let Us Drink to the Girl of My Dreams" (by L. Wolfe Gilbert and Abel Baer) with Arlen, Brian, Bruce, Cooper, Hall, Holmes, Newell, Peers and Wray. This latter sequence, along with other color footage, was subsequently edited out of *Paramount on Parade*'s abbreviated TV prints.

Leon Errol and JA in Paramount on Parade
(Paramount Pictures, 1930).

### The Return of Dr. Fu Manchu

(Paramount; 1930) 73 minutes.

Director: Rowland V. Lee. Screenplay: Florence Ryerson and Lloyd Corrigan. Based on the novel by Sax Rohmer. Cinematographer: Archie J. Stout. Sound: Eugene Merritt.

*Cast:* Warner Oland (*Dr. Fu Manchu*); O. P. Heggie (*Nayland Smith*); Jean Arthur (*Lia Eltham*); Neil Hamilton (*Jack Petrie*); Evelyn Hall (*Lady Agatha Bailey*); William Austin (*Sylvester Wadsworth*); Margaret Fealy (*Lady Helen Bartley*); Shayle Gardiner (*Inspector Harding*); Evelyn Selbie (*Fai Lo*); David Dunbar (*Lawrence*); Tetsu Komai (*Chang*); Toyo Fujita (*Ah Ling*); Ambrose Barker *(Reporter)*.

*The Film*: Consistent with its 1929 forerunner, *The Return of Dr. Fu Manchu* reunited a brunette Jean Arthur with Warner Oland, Neil Hamilton and O. P. Heggie in more evil Oriental hokum in a similar plotline, but with some added comic relief. This time out, Rowland V. Lee's direction seems tighter and the performances more natural. The *New York Times* found Arthur and Hamilton "acceptable," but liked Oland better in *The Mysterious Dr. Fu Manchu*. Although seemingly killed off at the conclusion of this 1930 melodrama, the character of Dr. Fu would return the following year in *Daughter of the Dragon*, but without Jean Arthur.

Neil Hamilton and JA in The Return of Dr. Fu Manchu
(Paramount Pictures, 1930).

### Danger Lights

(RKO Radio; 1930) 73 minutes. (Re-released in late-1930 in a wide-screen version at 87 minutes).

Director: George B. Seitz. Producer: William LeBaron; Supervision and Associate Producer: Myles Connolly; Screenplay: James Ashmore

Creelman. Cinematographer: Karl Struss. Art Director/Costumes: Max Ree. Editor: Archie F. Marshek. Photographic Effects: Lloyd Knechtel. Sound: Clem Portman. Technical Advisor: Walter W. St. Clair. Filmed in the 63.5mm Spoor-Berggren Natural Vision Process.

*Cast:* Louis Wolheim (*Dan Thorn*); Robert Armstrong (*Larry Doyle*); Jean Arthur (*Mary Ryan*); Hugh Herbert (*Professor*); Frank Sheridan (*Ed Ryan*); Robert Edeson (*Engineer*); Alan Roscoe (*General Manager*); William P. Burt (*Chief Dispatcher*); James Farley (*Joe Geraghty*).

*The Film*: In the first of a two-picture loan-out to RKO, Jean Arthur had yet another routine heroine role in yet another movie melodrama. This time, she's engaged to Louis Wolheim, but in love with Robert Armstrong who, in the film's climax, executes a daring locomotive run to Chicago to save the injured Wolheim.

This railroad yarn made little impression upon its initial August, 1930 presentation, but a November re-release in the innovational Spoor-Berggren Natural Vision Process, offered a widescreen 3-D illusion that attracted greater press attention and renewed audience interest. Due to prohibitive costs, RKO abandoned the process soon thereafter.

Robert Armstrong, JA and Louis Wolheim in Danger Lights
(RKO Radio Pictures, 1930).

### The Silver Horde

(RKO Radio; 1930) 75 minutes.
Director: George Archainbaud. Producer: William Le Baron. Associate Producer: William Sistrom. Screenplay: Wallace Smith. Based on the novel by Rex Beach. Art Director/Costumes: Max Ree. Cinematographers: Leo Tover and John W.Doyle. Editor: Otto Ludwig. Assistant Director: Thomas Atkins. Sound: Clem Portman.

*Cast:* Evelyn Brent (*Cherry Malotte*); Louis Wolheim (*George Balt*); Joel McCrea (*Boyd Emerson*); Raymond Hatton (*Fraser*); Jean Arthur (*Mildred Wayland*); Blanche Sweet (*Queenie*); Gavin Gordon (*Fred Marsh*); Purnell Pratt (*Wayne Wayland*); William Davidson (*Thomas Hilliard*); Ivan Linow (*Svenson*).

*The Film*: This was a remake of the 1909 Rex Beach novel about Alaska's salmon fishing industry first produced by Goldwyn Pictures in 1920 with Myrtle Stedman and Curtis Cooksey. In the RKO version, Jean Arthur had the thankless supporting role of a snobbish society girl who understandably loses fledgling cannery owner Joel McCrea to reformed loose-woman Evelyn Brent. Some effective action scenes, including the documentary-like footage of a cannery's operations, help compensate for an uneven, if entertaining, melodrama in which Arthur gives an irritatingly whiny performance. In a small part, silent star Blanche Sweet made her final screen appearance. This was the first leading role for up-and-coming star Joel McCrea. The *New York Times* thought the movie "dull and trivial."

JA and Evelyn Brent in The Silver Horde
(RKO Radio Pictures, 1930).

## The Gang Buster

(Paramount; 1931) 65 minutes.

Director: A. Edward Sutherland. Scenario and Story: Percy Heath. Dialogue: Joseph L. Mankiewicz. Cinematographer: Harry Fischbeck. Editor: Jane Loring. Sound: Harold M. McNiff. Music: John Leipold.

*Cast:* Jack Oakie (*Charlie "Cyclone" Case*); Jean Arthur (*Sylvia Martine*); William "Stage" Boyd (*"Sudden" Mike Slade*); Wynne Gibson (*Zella Cameron*); William Morris (*Andrew Martine*); Francis McDonald (*Pete Caltek*); Tom Kennedy (*"Gopher" Brant*); Albert Conti (*Carlo*); Harry

Stubbs (*Faulkner*); Ernie Adams (*Sammy*); Constantin Romanoff (*Otto*); Pat Harmon (*McGintey*); Joseph Girard (*Lieutenant*); Eddie Dunn (*Taxi Driver*); Arthur Hoyt (*Telephone Informant*).

*The Film:* This pleasantly entertaining satire on gangland melodramas cast Arthur as a kidnap victim who's eventually rescued from hoodlums by insurance salesman Oakie. Enjoyable performances by the two stars, along with chief villain Boyd, were well executed under the energetic direction of A. Edward Sutherland. And while the dialogue turned out by fledgling writer Joseph L. Mankiewicz could hardly anticipate the sparkle of his late-Forties scripts for *A Letter to Three Wives* and *All About Eve*, it was already a few notches above the average for 1931.

In what was surely her best part since *The Saturday Night Kid*, Jean Arthur won kudos from *Variety* for playing "a difficult role with easy grace."

## The Virtuous Husband

(aka: *What Wives Don't Want*) (Universal; 1931) 75 minutes.
Director: Vin Moore. Producer: Carl Laemmle Jr. Associate Producer: Albert de Mond. Screenplay: Dale Van Every. Adaptation: Edward Luddy and C. Jerome Horwin. Dialogue: Fred Niblo Jr. Based on the play *Apron Strings* by Dorrance Davis. Cinematographer: Jerome Ash. Art Director: Paul Roe Crowley. Editors: Harry W. Lieb and Arthur Hilton. Sound: C. Roy Hunter.
*Cast:* Elliott Nugent (*Daniel Curtis*); Jean Arthur (*Barbara Olwell*); Betty Compson (*Inez Wakefield*); J. C. Nugent (*John Olwell*); Alison Skipworth (*Eleanor Olwell*); Tully Marshall (*Ezra Hunniwell*); Eva McKenzie (*Hester*); Willie Best (*Loftus*).

*The Film:* Her first of two 1931 loan-outs to Universal Pictures cast Arthur as an annoyed bride who's forced to cope with the mother complex of her new husband (Nugent). It seems that his late parent left him a stack of letters to help guide him through life's challenges. Her role gave the actress few challenges, yet the *New York Times* found her performance "pleasing," and *Variety* singled her out to say: "Miss Arthur makes a slightly better showing here than in other recent assignments, despite material none too actor-proof."

J. C. Nugent, Alison Skipworth, Elliot Nugent, JA, Eva McKenzie and Betty Compson in The Virtuous Husband (Universal Pictures, 1931).

## The Lawyer's Secret

(Paramount; 1931) 65 minutes.

Directors: Louis Gasnier and Max Marcin. Associate Producer: David O. Selznick. Screenplay: Lloyd Corrigan and Max Marcin. Story: James Hilary Finn. Cinematographer: Arthur Todd. Sound: J. A. Goodrich.

*Cast:* Clive Brook (*Drake Norris*); Charles Rogers (*Laurie Roberts*); Richard Arlen (*Joe Hart*); Fay Wray (*Kay Roberts*); Jean Arthur (*Beatrice Stevens*); Francis McDonald (*The Weasel*); Harold Goodwin (*Madame X*); Syd Saylor (*Red*); Lawrence LaMarr (*Tom*); Robert Perry (*Baldy*); Wilbur Mack (*District Attorney*).

*The Film:* In the last film under her Paramount contract, Jean Arthur played the desperate girl friend of condemned-but-innocent sailor Richard Arlen. This multi-star melodrama about legal ethics and justice offers an effectively underplayed performance from the fifth-billed Arthur, in contrast to the emotional overacting going on all around her. The press paid little attention to *The Lawyer's Secret*, although the *New York Times'* Mordaunt Hall allowed that "Jean Arthur and Fay Wray add a certain luster to the feminine roles." Ironically, neither actress would have her contract renewed.

## Ex-Bad Boy

(aka: *His Temporary Affair*) (Universal; 1931) 76 minutes.

Director: Vin Moore. Screenplay: Dale Van Every and Fred Niblo Jr. Based on the play *The Whole Town's Talking* by Anita Loos and John Emerson. Cinematographer: Jerome Ash. Sound: C. Roy Hunter.

*Cast:* Robert Armstrong (*Chester Binney*); Jean Arthur (*Ethel Simmons*); Lola Lane (*Letta Lardo*); George Brent (*Donald Swift*); Jason Robards (*Roger Shields*); Grayce Hampton (*Mrs. Simmons*); Mary Doran (*Sadie Bloom*); Eddie Kane (*Theatre Manager*); Edward Hearn (*Assistant Manager*); Spencer Charters (*Henry Simmons*); Tony Stakenau (*Trainer*).

*The Film:* Despite being based on a play called *The Whole Town's Talking*, this movie bears no connection to Jean Arthur's 1935 Columbia picture of the same title. Instead, *Ex-Bad Boy* was an unpretentious little farce, reuniting her with *Danger Lights'* Robert Armstrong, as a paint-firm executive who invents a colorful past for himself to impress small-town-girl Arthur. In a cast that also included future leading man George Brent in a supporting role, third billed Lola Lane made the biggest splash as a visiting Hollywood star jokingly named "Letta Lardo."

Jason Robards Sr., JA and Robert Armstrong in Ex-Bad Boy
(Universal Pictures, 1931).

### The Past of Mary Holmes

(RKO Radio; 1933) 70 minutes.

Director: Harlan Thompson. Executive Producer: David O. Selznick. Associate Producer: Bartlett Cormack. Screenplay: Sam Ornitz, Edward Marion Dix and Edward Doherty. Based on the novel *The Goose Woman* by Rex Beach. Cinematographer: Charles Rosher. Editor: Charles L. Kimball. Art Directors: Van Nest Polglase and Al Herman. Sound: Hugh McDowell Jr.

*Cast:* Helen MacKellar (*Mary Holmes*); Eric Linden (*Geoffrey Holmes*); Jean Arthur (*Joan Hoyt*); Richard "Skeets" Gallagher (*Ben Pratt*); Ivan Simpson (*Jacob Riggs*); Clay Clement (*G. K. Ethridge*); Franklin Parker (*Brooks*); Edward Nugent (*Flanagan*); Roscoe Ates (*Klondike*); J. Carrol Naish (*Gary Kent*); John Sheehan (*Tom Kincaid*); Rochelle Hudson (*Betty*); Jane Darwell (*Woman*).

*The Film:* Rex Beach's novel *The Goose Woman* had originally reached the screen in 1925, under that title, when Universal filmed it with Louise Dresser, Jack Pickford and Constance Bennett in the roles played here by Helen MacKellar, Eric Linden and Jean Arthur. The latter portrays an actress who loves Linden, the son of embittered "goose woman" MacKellar, a former opera singer who believes his birth to blame for her losing her voice years earlier. When the young man's falsely accused of murder, mother testifies against son, until the eventual triumph of justice.

Arthur had been off the screen for nearly two years when *The Past of Mary Holmes* was released in the spring of 1933. *Variety* noted the "suitable support" of Arthur and character actor Ivan Simpson, while the *New York Times* wrote, "Jean Arthur is better than usual as the girl."

Ivan Simpson, JA and Helen MacKellar in The Past of Mary Holmes
(RKO Radio Pictures, 1933).

## Get That Venus

(aka: *The Unwanted Venus*) (Regent Pictures; 1933) Six reels.
Director: Grover Lee (aka Arthur Varney). Screenplay: Val Valentine. Based on the story "The Mystic Fool" by Gerald Villiers Stuart. Cinematography: Nick Rogalli and Marcel Picard. Assistant Director: Walter Sheridan.
*Cast:* Ernest Truex (*Tom Wilson*); Jean Arthur (*Margaret Rendleby*); Harry Davenport (*Mr. Rendleby*); Tom Howard (*Joe Smiley*); Molly O'Day (*Belle*); Herbert Rawlinson (*Editor Nash*); May Vokes (*Mrs. Murphy*); Stanley Harrison (*Fishkins*); Olga Anson (*Georgina Van Aster*). With Donald MacBride and Wesley Barry.
*The Film*: The most obscure of all Jean Arthur's talkies was produced independently during the early summer of 1933 by the British-financed Starmark Productions, shooting at the Metropolitan Studios in Fort Lee, New Jersey. Using actors from the New York stage, this low-budget movie

had to do with a stolen painting of Venus, with Arthur and Ernest Truex cast as the unlikely romantic leads. Research reveals no records of any theatrical release, nor were there any reviews, not even in the Hollywood trade publications. However, an 8mm print was available for film rental in the Sixties.

## *Whirlpool*

(Columbia; 1934) 73 minutes.
Director: Roy William Neill. Screenplay: Dorothy Howell and Ethel Hill. Story: Howard Emmett Rogers. Cinematographers: Benjamin Cline, Joseph August and John Stumar. Editor: Richard Cahoon. Sound: Glenn Rominger. Special Effects: John Hoffman.

*Cast:* Jack Holt (*Buck Rankin*); Jean Arthur (*Sandra Morrison*); Allen Jenkins (*Mac*); Donald Cook (*Bob Andrews*); Lila Lee (*Helen Morrison*); Rita LaRoy (*Thelma*); John Miljan (*Barney Gaige*); Willard Robertson (*Judge Morrison*); Ward Bond (*Farley*); Oscar Apfel (*Editor*); Gino Corrado (*Tony*); Al Hill (*Spike*); John M. Sullivan (*Judge*).

*The Film:* In her first film for the then-unprestigious Columbia Pictures, Jean Arthur played a reporter covering a criminal case who interviews a racketeer (Jack Holt). In the melodramatic course of events, it turns out that he's actually her father, long imprisoned and believed dead. Eventually, Holt is driven to shoot his blackmailer (John Miljan), before turning the gun on himself.

Contracted for independently, because Arthur liked the script, *Whirlpool* moved *Variety* to call it "well above fair in audience appeal," adding " . . . for high sympathetic and heart interest, Jean Arthur is what the doctor ordered." In the New York *Herald Tribune*, Howard Barnes cited her "brilliant and thoroughly plausible portrayal of a difficult role." Most importantly, Columbia was sufficiently impressed with her work in *Whirlpool* to offer a long-term contract.

JA and Lila Lee in Whirlpool (Columbia Pictures, 1934).

### *The Defense Rests*

(Columbia; 1934) 70 minutes.

Director: Lambert Hillyer. Screenplay and Story: Jo Swerling. Cinematographer: Joseph August. Editor: John Rawlins. Sound: Edward Bernds.

*Cast:* Jack Holt (*Matthew Mitchell*); Jean Arthur (*Joan Hayes*); Nat Pendleton (*Rocky*); Arthur Hohl (Lila Lee, *James Randolph*); Raymond Walburn (*Austin*); Harold Huber (*Castro*); Robert Gleckler (*Gentry*); Sarah Padden (*Mrs. Evans*); Shirley Grey (*Mabel Wilson*) Raymond Hatton (*Nick*); Ward Bond (*Good*); Vivian Oakland (*Mrs. Ballou*); Donald Meek (*Fogg*); John Wray (*Cooney*); Samuel S. Hinds (*Dean Adams*); J. Carrol Naish (*Ballou*); Selmer Jackson (*Duffy*); Bess Flowers (*Receptionist*); Mary Gordon (*Scrub Woman*).

*The Film:* Another Columbia melodrama, this time with Arthur as an idealistic law-school graduate who opposes the tactics of underworld lawyer Holt. Eventually, she reforms him and wins his heart, despite their age differences. The critics had more praise for the script and Lambert Hillyer's well paced direction than for the movie's star performances.

Jack Holt and JA in The Defense Rests
(Columbia Pictures, 1934).

## The Most Precious Thing in Life
(Columbia; 1934) 68 minutes.

Director: Lambert Hillyer. Screenplay: Ethel Hill and Dore Schary. Story: Travis Ingham. Cinematographer: John Stumar. Editor: Richard Cahoon. Sound: Glenn Rominger and Lambert Day. Assistant Director: Robert Margolis.

*Cast*: Richard Cromwell (*Chris Kelsey*); Jean Arthur (*Ellen Holmes*); Donald Cook (*Bob Kelsey*); Anita Louise (*Patty O'Day*); Mary Forbes (*Mrs. Kelsey*); Jane Darwell (*Mrs. O'Day*); Ben Alexander (*Gubby Gerhart*); John Wray (*Carter*); Ward Bond (*Coach Smith*); Samuel S. Hinds (*The Dean*); Dutch Hendrian (*Assistant Coach*); Paul Stanton (*Mr. Kelsey*); Maidel Turner (*Dean's Wife*); Heinie Conklin (*Porter*); Ray Cooke (*College Boy*).

*The Film*: Affording Arthur the opportunity to age 20 years, this soap opera centered on a middle-aged lady who becomes a college cleaning-woman to be near her son (Cromwell), a cocky student who knows nothing of her real identity. Mindful of other screen actresses who'd recently portrayed time—spanning roles (e.g., Irene Dunne in *Cimarron*; Norma Shearer in *Strange Interlude*), Arthur relished playing this part. Unfortunately, she was at her best in the movie's early scenes, where she's more convincing as a young woman. The scenes of her aging occur during a short montage sequence, and her makeup isn't sufficiently detailed to make her mature character believable. *Variety* noted that, while Arthur wasn't physically convincing, "she troupes the assignment nicely and often with a note of sincerity."

### The Whole Town's Talking

(aka: *Passport to Fame*) (Columbia; 1935) 95 minutes.

Director: John Ford. Producer: Lester Cowan. Screenplay: Jo Swerling and Robert Riskin. Based on the story "Jail Breaker" by W. R. Burnett. Cinematographer: Joseph August. Editor: Viola Lawrence. Assistant Director: Wilbur McGaugh. Sound: Paul Neal.

*Cast:* Edward G. Robinson (*Arthur Ferguson "Jonesy" Jones/Killer Mannion*); Jean Arthur (*Wilhelmina "Bill" Clark*); Arthur Hohl (*Det. Sgt. Mike Boyle*); James Donlan (*Det. Sgt. Pat Howe*); Arthur Byron (*District Attorney Spencer*); Wallace Ford (*Healy*); Donald Meek (*Hoyt*); Etienne Girardot (*Seaver*); Edward Brophy (*Bugs Martin*); Paul Harvey (*J. G. Carpenter*); J. Farrell MacDonald (*Warden*); Effie Ellsler (*Aunt Agatha*); Robert Emmet O'Connor (*Lt. Mack*); John Wray (*Nick*); Joseph Sauers/Joe Sawyer (*Harry*); Frank Sheridan (*Russell*); Clarence Hummel Wilson (*President of Chamber of Commerce*); Virginia Pine (*Seaver's Secretary*); Ferdinand Munier (*Mayor*); Cornelius Keefe (*Radio Man*); Francis Ford (*Reporter at Dock*); Lucille Ball (*Girl*); Robert E. Homans (*Detective*); Grace Hayle (*Sob Sister*); Emmett Vogan (*Reporter*); Bess Flowers *(Secretary);* Mary Gordon *(Landlady).*

Edward G. Robinson, Arthur Byron, Arthur Hohl and JA in The Whole Town's Talking (Columbia Pictures, 1935).

*The Film*: John Ford, who directed Jean Arthur's motion picture debut in *Cameo Kirby* 12 years earlier, was the guiding force behind this delightful comic melodrama. And, if its overall atmosphere seems more Capra-esque than Ford-like, attribution is undoubtedly due Robert Riskin, a frequent Capra collaborator (*It Happened One Night*) who coauthored this screenplay with Jo Swerling. Edward G. Robinson has the juicy role of a mousy advertising clerical worker who happens to be the spitting image of a murderous mobster (also played by Robinson). Arthur is the self-possessed secretary, much admired by the clerk, who helps him foil the gang and become a public hero. The sequence in which she poses as a gun moll to save colleague Robinson from the mob's violence is a forerunner of the screwball comedy in which she'd later excel.

Arthur's role is considerably smaller than Robinson's and, in the hands of a lesser actress, could have been far less memorable. In *The Whole Town's Talking*, there's little sign of her vapid, sometimes whiny ingénues of five years earlier. Instead, the actress projects a brassy self-confidence that nevertheless maintains a sympathetic quality with which audiences could readily identify. *Photoplay* magazine remarked on her "excellent support," while the *New York Times* said "For separate applause it is possible to isolate Jean Arthur as the hardboiled young woman who is the object of Jonesy's timid affection."

After praising Robinson's virtuoso dual performance, *Variety* turned the spotlight to his leading lady, noting the value of her recent stage experience:

> "She will get other opportunities as a result of this auspicious baptism in flippancy. Whoever guided her in the metamorphosis was canny in reading production trends."

### Party Wire

(Columbia; 1935) 69 minutes.

Director: Erle C. Kenton. Producer: Robert North. Screenplay: John Howard Lawson and Ethel Mill. Based on the novel by Bruce Manning and Vera Caspary. Cinematographer: Allen Siegler. Editor: Viola Lawrence. Art Director: Stephen Goosson. Sound: William Hamilton.

*Cast:* Jean Arthur (*Marge Oliver*); Victor Jory (*Matthew Putnam*); Helen Lowell (*Nettie Putnam*); Charley Grapewin (*Will Oliver*); Robert Allen (*Roy Daniels*); Clara Blandick (*Mathilda Sherman*); Geneva Mitchell (*Irene Sherman*); Maude Eburne (*Clara West*); Matt McHugh (*Bert West*); Oscar Apfel (*Tom Sherman*); Robert Middlemass (*Judge Stephenson*); Edward LeSaint (*Mason*); Charles Middleton (*Johnson*); Harvey Clark (*Croft*); Walter Brennan (*Paul*); Grace Hayle (*Eleanor*); Joe Smith Marba (*Joe*); Dorothy Bay (*Rebecca*); Emerson Treacy (*Martin*); George C. Pearce (*Country Doctor*).

*The Film:* Before *The Whole Town's Talking* could present a new, more exciting Jean Arthur to the public, this unpretentious programmer was produced as another of the typical lineup of B-pictures ground out by the studios to help fulfill the needs of double-bill distribution in that era. In *Party Wire*, small-town gossip erroneously brands Arthur a "fallen woman," jeopardizing her future with the local most-eligible bachelor (Victor Jory). But, of course, the rumors turn out to be false, and all ends happily for the film's protagonists.

If nothing else, *Party Wire* deserves notice for being the first movie to give Arthur top billing. *Variety* called it "an entertaining comedy which will satisfy the family trade."

Robert Allen and JA in Party Wire
(Columbia Pictures, 1935).

## *Public Hero #1*

(Metro-Goldwyn-Mayer; 1935) 91 minutes.

Director: J. Walter Ruben. Producer: Lucian Hubbard. Screenplay: Wells Root. Story: J. Walter Ruben and Wells Root. Cinematographer: Gregg Toland. Editor: Frank Sullivan. Art Directors: Cedric Gibbons, Lionel Banks and Edwin B. Willis. Costumes: Dolly Tree. Music: Edward Ward. Sound: Douglas Shearer.

*Cast:* Lionel Barrymore (*Dr. Josiah Glass*); Jean Arthur (*Maria "Terry" O'Reilly*); Chester Morris (*Jeff Crane*); Joseph Calleia (*Sonny Black*); Paul Kelly (*Duff*); Lewis Stone (*Warden Alcott*); Sam Baker (*Mose*); Paul Hurst (*Rufe Parker*); George E. Stone (*Butch*); John Kelly (*Truck Driver*); Selmer Jackson (*Simpson*); Lawrence Wheat (*Andrews*); Cora Sue Collins (*Little Girl*); Lillian Harmer (*Mrs. Higgins*); Jonathan Hale (*Prison Board Member*); Arthur Housman (*Drunk*); Bert Roach (*Bus Passenger*); Frank McGlynn Jr., James Flavin, Gladden James, Pat O'Malley and Anderson Lawler (*Federal Agents*); Zeffie Tilbury (*Deaf Woman*); Frank Darien (*Dr. Hale*); Greta Meyer (*Housekeeper*); Walter Brennan (*Farmer*).

*The Film:* Due to his longtime prestige at Metro-Goldwyn-Mayer, character actor Lionel Barrymore received top billing in this uneven blend of comedy and action melodrama, despite the brevity of his footage. The picture's real star is Chester Morris, as a G-Man who infiltrates a gang by passing as one of their kind. As the flippant sister of gang boss Joseph Calleia, Arthur manages a measure of rambunctious romance with tough guy Morris.

Released several months after her breakthrough performance in *The Whole Town's Talking*, this movie garnered even more laudatory notices for its female star. *Photoplay* reported, "Jean Arthur establishes herself firmly as the leading flip-but-serious ingénue with all the answers." *Movie Classic* magazine opined, "Jean Arthur, who scored a minor triumph in *The Whole Town's Talking*, scores a major one as the heroine of this piece." And the *New York Times*, after dubbing *Public Hero #1* "a rattling good show," zeroed in on the work of Arthur and the always sinister Joseph Calleia: "Jean Arthur, whom you may recall for her breezy excellence in *The Whole Town's Talking*, is as refreshing a change from the routine it-girl as Mr. Calleia is in his own department."

### *Diamond Jim*

(Universal; 1935) 93 minutes.

Director: A. Edward Sutherland. Producer: Edmund Grainger. Screenplay: Preston Sturges. Adaptation: Doris Malloy and Harry Clork. Based on the book by Parker Morell. Cinematographer: George Robinson. Photographic Effects: John P. Fulton. Editor: Daniel Mandell. Art Director: Charles D. Hall. Costumes: Vera West. Music: Franz Waxman. Sound: Gilbert Kurland.

*Cast:* Edward Arnold (*"Diamond Jim" Brady*); Jean Arthur (*Jane Mathews/ Emma Perry*); Binnie Barnes (*Lillian Russell*); Cesar Romero (*Jerry Richardson*); Eric Blore (*Sampson Fox*); Hugh O'Connell (*Charles B. Horsley*); George Sidney (*Pawnbroker*); Robert McWade (*Mr. Moore*); Charles Sellon (*Station Agent Touchey*); Henry Kolker (*Bank President*); William Demarest (*Harry Hill*); Albert Conti (*Jeweler*); Armand Kaliz (*Jewelry Salesman*); Tully Marshall (*Minister*); Purnell Pratt (*Doctor*); Helen Brown (*Brady's Mother*); Bill Hoolahahn (*John L. Sullivan*); Fred Kelsey (*Secretary*); Otis Harlan (*Drunk*); Lew Kelley (*Bartender*); Irving Bacon (*Train Passenger*); Robert Emmet O'Connor (*Brady's Father*); Greta Meyer (*Masseuse*); Eily Malyon (*Organist*); Maidel Turner (*Mrs. Perry*); Wade Boteler (*Mill Foreman*).

*The Film:* On loan to Universal, Arthur enjoyed a dual role in this handsomely produced but bogus pseudo-biography of millionaire "Diamond Jim" Brady, with the emphasis on his romantic relationships. As Brady,

Edward Arnold and JA in Diamond Jim (Universal Pictures, 1935).

118

character-leading-man Edward Arnold skillfully dominates the movie and garnered critical admiration. Nevertheless, the press took notice of *Diamond Jim*'s fellow cast members, as well. *Variety* reported, "Arnold is admirably supported by Jean Arthur and Binnie Barnes, both first-rate troupers, as well as decorative."

As two different women, both of whom reject Brady's attentions, Arthur briefly portrays a Southern coquette and later a calculating social climber with a past. Since her distinctive voice is poorly dubbed by an uncredited performer for her earlier role, there's unintentional humor in that one short scene. The film's reviewers were generally critical of Preston Sturges' screenplay and its liberal adaptation of Parker Morell's original biography. Once again, Hollywood chose to replace historical fact with romantic fiction.

### The Public Menace

(Columbia; 1935) 73 minutes.

Director: Erle C. Kenton. Screenplay and Story: Ethel Hill and Lionel Houser. Cinematographer: Henry Freulich. Editor: Gene Milford. Costumes: Murray Mayer. Sound: Glenn Rominger.

*Cast*: Jean Arthur (*Cassie*); George Murphy (*Red Foster*); Douglass Dumbrille (*Tonelli*); George McKay (*Dildy*); Robert Middlemass (*Frentrup*); Victor Kilian (*Joe*); Charles C. Wilson (*First Detective*); Gene Morgan (*Cox*); Murray Alper (*Stiglitz*); Shirley Grey (*Mimi*); Bradley Page (*Louis*); Arthur Rankin (*Tommy*); Thurston Hall (*Captain of the Ocean Liner*); Fred Kelsey (*Mike*); Clarence Muse (*Janitor*); Selmer Jackson (*Chief Steward*); Emmett Vogan (*Bail Bond Broker*); George Cleveland (*Pilot*).

*The Film*: In an era where gangsters, whether serious or comic, continued to provide popular material for motion pictures, Columbia now incorporated them for humorous effect into *The Public Menace*, the last minor programmer Jean Arthur would make for that studio. Here, she plays a manicurist who weds reporter George Murphy and gets inadvertently mixed up with a mob governed by the perennially sinister Douglass Dumbrille. *Variety* thought Arthur "particularly good," thanks partly to Erle C. Kenton's "deft direction" of a smart screenplay by Ethel Hill and Lionel Houser.

JA, Douglass Dumbrille and George McKay in The Public Menace
(Columbia Pictures, 1935).

## *If You Could Only Cook*

(Columbia; 1935) 70 minutes.

Director: William A. Seiter. Associate Producer: Everett Riskin. Screenplay: Howard J. Green and Gertrude Purcell. Story: F. Hugh Herbert. Cinematographer: John Stumar. Editor: Gene Harlick. Art Director: Stephen Goosson. Costumes: Samuel Lange. Sound: George Cooper.

*Cast*: Herbert Marshall (*Jim Buchanan*); Jean Arthur (*Joan Hawthorne*); Leo Carrillo (*Mike Rossini*); Lionel Stander (*Flash*); Alan Edwards (*Bob Reynolds*); Frieda Inescort (*Evelyn Fletcher*); Gene Morgan (*Al*); Ralf Harolde (*Swig*); Matt McHugh (*Pete*); Richard Powell (*Testy*); Jonathan Hale (*Henry*); Arthur Hohl (*Police Detective*); Constantin Romanoff (*Lefty*); Edward McWade (*Justice of the Peace*); Pierre Watkin (*Mr. Balderson*); Russell Hicks (*Dillon*); Bess Flowers (*Laura*).

*The Film*: Once again, gangsters figure into the plot of a Jean Arthur movie, this time to whimsically amusing effect as an unemployed young career woman meets an auto tycoon (Herbert Marshall) on a park bench. Believing he's also out of work, she convinces him to help her pose as a butler-and-cook married couple, who find employment—and eventually romance—in what turns

Leo Carrillo and JA in If You Could Only Cook (Columbia Pictures, 1935).

out to be the mobster household of Leo Carrillo and Lionel Stander. The story's "fun" potential proved more entertaining in theory than in execution, yet Columbia had enough faith in this product to release *If You Could Only Cook* as their late-December holiday presentation for 1935. And the press continued to admire Jean Arthur. *Variety* named hers as the film's "standout performance," and concluded, "Where she doesn't fetch 'em with that fine flair for comedy, the charm she lends to the romantic episodes will do the trick." In his astute retrospective coverage of the movie's DVD release, the *New York Times*' Dave Kehr wrote: "Apart from her distinctive, raspy voice, it's difficult to detect any self-conscious technique in Arthur's superbly naturalistic work. If anything, she often seems to be moving more slowly and speaking with more deliberation than her co-stars, an unobtrusive way of assuming the emotional focus and moral center of the action."

## Mr. Deeds Goes to Town

(Columbia; 1936) 115 minutes.

Director/Producer: Frank Capra. Screenplay: Robert Riskin. Based on the story "Opera Hat" by Clarence Budington Kelland. Cinematographer: Joseph Walker. Editor: Gene Havlick. Art Director: Stephen Goosson. Special Effects: E. Roy Davidson. Costumes: Samuel Lange. Musical Direction: Howard Jackson. Sound: Edward Bernds.

*Cast*: Gary Cooper (*Longfellow Deeds*); Jean Arthur (*Louise "Babe" Bennett*); George Bancroft (*MacWade*); Lionel Stander (*Cornelius Cobb*); Douglass Dumbrille (*John Cedar*); Raymond Walburn (*Walter*); H. B. Warner (*Judge May*); Ruth Donnelly (*Mabel Dawson*); Walter Catlett (*Morrow*); John Wray (*Farmer*); Margarete Matzenhauer (*Madame Pomponi*); Warren Hymer (*Bodyguard*); Muriel Evans (*Theresa*); Spencer Charters (*Mal*); Emma Dunn (*Mrs. Meredith*); Wyrley Birch (*Psychiatrist*); Arthur Hoyt (*Budington*); Stanley Andrews (*James Cedar*); Pierre Watkin (*Arthur Cedar*); Christian Rub (*Swenson*); Jameson Thomas (*Mr. Semple*); Mayo Methot (*Mrs. Semple*); Margaret Seddon (*Jane Faulkner*); Margaret McWade (*Amy Faulkner*); Russell Hicks (*Dr. Malcolm*); Gustav von Seyffertitz (*Dr. Frazier*); Edward Le Saint (*Dr. Fosdick*); Charles Lane (*Hallor*); Irving Bacon (*Frank*); Edward Gargan (*Bodyguard*); Paul Hurst (*Deputy*); Franklin Pangborn (*Tailor*); Paul Porcasi (*Italian*); George "Gabby" Hayes (*Shorty*); George Meeker (*Henneberry*); Barnett Parker (*Butler*); Bud Flanagan/Dennis O'Keefe (*Reporter*); Ann Doran (*Girl on Bus*); Edwin Maxwell (*Douglas*); Billy Bevan (*Cabby*); Dale Van Sickel (*Lawyer*).

*The Film*: The iconic Frank Capra produced and directed this comedy gem, the first of Jean Arthur's unqualified cinema classics. Not that she came by the role easily. Indeed, several other actresses were originally considered before Carole Lombard was signed to co-star with Gary Cooper. But then Lombard was offered the screwball comedy *My Man Godfrey*, opposite ex-husband William Powell at Universal, and she deserted the Capra project at the eleventh hour, after *Mr. Deeds* had already begun shooting. Although several well-known ladies were eager to work with Capra, he remained undecided until, as he tells it in his 1971 memoir *The Name Above the Title*, he happened to attend a Columbia screening of a Jack Holt movie that was probably *The Defense Rests*. As he describes it: "I had never seen the girl before. No, not a girl; a lovely young woman; simple, real, vibrant. And that voice! Low, husky—at times it broke pleasingly into the octaves like a thousand tinkling bells."

And thus luck would acquaint Frank Capra with Jean Arthur. One day he would fondly recall her as his favorite actress.

*Mr. Deeds Goes to Town* now represents what most classic-film buffs think of as a typical Capra picture: small-town guy inherits a fortune and relocates to the big city, where he's ridiculed by the press and victimized by officialdom—until he shrewdly learns to fight back (with strong female support) and defeat the opposing team.

In this prototype screenplay, winningly adapted from Clarence Budington Kelland's *Saturday Evening Post* story "Opera Hat" by the always-reliable Robert Riskin, Gary Cooper plays Vermonter

Christian Rub, Pierre Watkin, JA and George Bancroft in Mr Deeds Goes to Town (Columbia Pictures, 1936)

Longfellow Deeds, whose main pursuit is composing verses for greeting cards. When a distant relative leaves him $20-million, Deeds goes to New York to collect the bequest, and becomes so disenchanted with the opportunistic reception that greets him that he decides to concentrate on helping the needy. His plan to bestow farms on landless farmers meets with opposition from lawyers of his benefactor who try to get Deeds ruled insane to gain control of his windfall. Jean Arthur plays the cynical newspaper reporter who initially sets out to exploit Deeds before falling in love with him and helping establish his sanity. For Cooper, Longfellow Deeds was a perfect fit for his engaging but limited acting talents, firmly establishing him as the quintessential American hero. And for Arthur, embroidering on her breezy, flippant "Bill" Clark of *The Whole Town's Talking*, "Babe" Bennett proved a career landmark; in her 71$^{st}$ motion picture, the now-familiar Arthurian screen image was finally in full flower. Neither *Variety* nor the *New York Times*, both of which deemed the movie "pleasant," had any special words for Jean Arthur. But *Screenland* magazine's Delight Evans called her "brilliantly believable," and *Screen Book*'s reviewer thought that "Gary Cooper and Jean Arthur score the best performances of their careers . . . under the masterful direction of Frank Capra."

For 1936, *Mr. Deeds Goes to Town* was voted Best Picture by both the New York Film Critics and the National Board of Review. And it garnered five Academy Award nominations (including picture, actor, screenplay and sound), with its one statuette going to Best Director Capra.

### The Ex-Mrs. Bradford

(RKO; 1936) 80 minutes.

Director: Stephen Roberts. Associate Producer: Edward Kaufman. Screenplay: Anthony Veiller. Story: James Edward Grant. Cinematographer: J. Roy Hunt. Editor: Arthur Roberts. Art Directors: Van Nest Polglase and Perry Ferguson. Set Dresser: Darrell Silvera. Costumes: Bernard Newman. Music Director: Roy Webb. Sound: John L. Cass.

*Cast*: William Powell (*Dr. Lawrence Bradford*); Jean Arthur (*Paula Bradford*); James Gleason (*Inspector Corrigan*); Eric Blore (*Stokes*); Robert Armstrong (*Nick Martel*); Lila Lee (*Miss Prentiss*); Grant Mitchell (*Mr. Summers*); Erin O'Brien-Moore (*Mrs. Summers*); Ralph Moran (*Mr. Hutchins*); Lucile Gleason (*Mrs. Hutchins*); Frank M. Thomas (*Mike North*); Frankie Darro (*Spike Salsbury*); Frank Reicher (*Henry Strand*); Charles Richman (*Curtis*); John Sheehan (*Murphy*); Paul Fix (*Lou Pender*); Johnny Arthur (*Frankenstein*); James Donlan (*Cabby*); Spencer Charters (*Coroner*); Dorothy Granger (*Receptionist*); Stanley Blystone (*Police Radio Operator*); Syd Saylor (*Detective*); Rollo Lloyd (*Landlord*).

*The Film*: Jean Arthur enjoyed a congenial reunion, for the first time in six years, with her old Paramount teammate William Powell on loan-out to RKO for this Thin Man-like screwball comedy-mystery. It's about an urbane surgeon whose former spouse, like himself an amateur sleuth, involves him in a racetrack murder case centering on the death of a jockey. Although at times on the talky side, this was considered among the best of Hollywood's mid-Thirties trend toward carbon-copying Nick and Nora Charles, with sly humor to be found in *The Ex-Mrs. Bradford*'s climactic scene, in which Powell shows a room full of gathered suspects incriminating film he's secretly taken at the track.

The critical consensus approved of *The Ex-Mrs. Bradford*, with the *New York Times* lauding Arthur as "an amusing little clown who manages to be Mr. Powell's best friend and severest handicap without ever quite convincing us that she is just a nitwit."

### Adventure in Manhattan

(aka: *Manhattan Madness*) (Columbia: 1936) 73 minutes.
Director: Edward Ludwig. Associate Producer: Everett Riskin. Screenplay: Sidney Buchman, Harry Sauber and Jack Kirkland. Story: Joseph Krumgold. Based on the story "Purple and Fine Linen" by May Eginton. Cinematographer: Henry Freulich. Editor: Otto Meyer. Art Director: Stephen Goosson. Costumes: Bernard Newman. Musical Director: Morris Stoloff. Sound: Glen Rominger.
*Cast:* Jean Arthur (*Claire Peyton*); Joel McCrea (*George Melville*); Reginald Owen (*Blackton Gregory*); Thomas Mitchell (*Phil Bane*); Victor Kilian (*Mark Gibbs*); Jack Gallaudet (*McGuire*); Emmet Vogan (*Lorimer*); George Cooper (*Duncan*); Herman Bing (*Tim*); Robert Warwick (*Philip*); John Hamilton (*Head G-Man*); Barnett Parker (*John*); Billy Benedict (*Office Boy*); Bess Flowers (*Attendant*).
*The Film:* For this odd blend of comedy, mystery and melodrama, Jean Arthur was reunited with Joel McCrea, her *Silver Horde* co-star from 1930, albeit this time she had top billing and did not lose him to an on-screen rival. The story had served as a 1927 First National vehicle for silent star Corinne Griffith under the title *Three Hours*. In its Columbia remake, Arthur plays a stage actress who aids criminologist McCrea, who's working on a series of newspaper articles about a legendary thief. McCrea believes that a criminal, long believed dead, may still be alive and committing new crimes. Arthur even helps McCrea foil a bank robbery before the fact. And, of course, the two fall in love.

The film's convoluted script veers from this storyline to include sideline elements that only serve to underscore that the basic yarn needed padding. The fact that three people are credited with the screenplay reveals something about the problems inherent in putting such disparate material together.

Critics found all of this less than convincing, while crediting director Edward Ludwig and his cast for making a farfetched, disjointed movie look good in spite of its origins.

### More Than a Secretary

(Columbia; 1936) 77 minutes.

Director: Alfred E. Green. Associate Producer: Everett Riskin. Screenplay: Dale Van Every and Lynn Starling. Story: Ethel Hill and Aben Kandel. Based on the story "Safari in Manhattan" by Matt Taylor. Cinematographer: Henry Freulich. Editor: Al Clark. Art Director: Stephen Goosson. Costumes: Bernard Newman. Music: Morris Stoloff. Sound: Glenn Rominger.

*Cast*: Jean Arthur (*Carol Baldwin*); George Brent (*Fred Gilbert*); Lionel Stander (*Ernest*); Ruth Donnelly (*Helen Davis*); Reginald Denny (*Bill Houston*); Dorothea Kent (*Maizie West*); Charles Halton (*Mr. Crosby*); Geraldine Hall (*Enid*); Charles Irwin (*Mounted Policeman*); Myra Marsh (*Sour-Faced Woman*); Ann Merrill (*Betty*); William Bartlett (*Contortionist*); Tom Ricketts (*Henry*); Josephine McKim (*Gladys*); Dorothy Short (*Ann*).

*The Film:* George Brent, who'd had a secondary role in *Ex-Bad Boy* five years earlier, now served as Arthur's leading man in *More Than a Secretary*, a pleasant but minor comedy. She's the mousey owner of a secretarial establishment, and he's the editor of a health magazine who seems to be having trouble keeping secretaries on the job. When she's hired to solve the problem, she's mistaken for a job applicant and, attracted to Brent, accepts the position. With Arthur's help the magazine attains renewed success—until new stenographer Dorothea Kent enters the scene, and distracts Brent from both Arthur and the magazine.

JA and George Brent in More Than a Secretary (Columbia Pictures, 1936).

An expert cast and Alfred E. Green's firm direction helped, as did solid production values, but *More Than a Secretary*'s weak script made for only moderately pleasing entertainment. *Movie Mirror* opined that " . . . both Brent and Jean are in fine form."

### The Plainsman

(Paramount: 1937) 113 minutes.

Director/Producer: Cecil B. DeMille. Associate Producer: William H. Pine. Screenplay: Waldemar Young, Harold Lamb and Lynn Riggs. Based on the books *Wild Bill Hickok* by Frank J. Wilstach and *The Prince of Pistoleers* by Courtney Riley Cooper and Grover Jones, and material compiled by Jeanie Macpherson. Cinematographer: Victor Milner. Special Photographic Effects: Gordon Jennings, Farciot Edouart and Dewey Wrigley. Editor: Anne Bauchens. Art Directors: Hans Dreier and Roland Anderson. Set

Decoration: A. E. Freudeman. Costumes: Natalie Visart, Dwight Franklin and Joe De Yong. Music: George Antheil. Musical Direction: Boris Morros. Sound: Harry M. Lindgren and Louis Mesenkop. Assistant Director: Richard Harlan.

*Cast*: Gary Cooper (*Wild Bill Hickok*); Jean Arthur (*Calamity Jane*); James Ellison (*Buffalo Bill Cody*); Charles Bickford (*John Lattimer*); Helen Burgess (*Louisa Cody*); Porter Hall (*Jack McCall*); Paul Harvey (*Yellow Hand*); Victor Varconi (*Painted Horse*); John Miljan (*Gen. George A. Custer*); Frank McGlynn Sr. (*Abraham Lincoln*); Granville Bates (*Van Ellyn*); Frank Albertson (*Young Trooper*); Purnell Pratt (*Captain Wood*); Fred Kohler (*Jake*); Pat Moriarty (*Sergeant McGinnis*); Charles Judels (*Tony, the Barber*); Harry Woods (*Quartermaster Sergeant*); Anthony Quinn (*Cheyenne Warrior*); Francis McDonald (*River Gambler*); George Ernst (*A Boy*); George MacQuarrie (*General Merritt*); George "Gabby" Hayes (*Breezy*); Fuzzy Knight (*Dave*); Francis Ford (*A Veteran*); Irving Bacon (*Soldier*); Edgar Dearing (*Custer's Messenger*); Edwin Maxwell (*Stanton*); Arthur Aylesworth, Douglas Wood and George Cleveland (*Van Elllyn's Assistants*); Lona Andre (*Southern Belle*); Leila McIntyre (*Mary Todd Lincoln*); Harry Stubbs (*John F. Usher*); Bud Flanagan/Dennis O'Keefe (*Second Man*); Noble Johnson (*First Indian with Painted Horse*).

Gary Cooper and JA in The Plainsman (Paramount Pictures, 1937).

*The Film*: Cecil B. DeMille's glorified, epic conception of the world of Wild Bill Hickok and Calamity Jane characteristically bore little resemblance to the facts of 19th-century Western history. DeMille was a showman who always opted for entertainment over documentary realism. In *The Plainsman*, he chose to synthesize the romance and adventure of pioneer America, serving up the results in a stirring blend of folklore and movie-star glamour that reinforced the public appeal of Gary Cooper and Jean Arthur in roles far removed from their recent teaming in *Mr. Deeds Goes to Town*. In this Western setting, Cooper loses his trademarked awkwardness, and Arthur responds enthusiastically to boots, trousers and a man-taming bullwhip. Of course, DeMille presents her as a way-too-glamorous Calamity Jane, with lipstick, mascaraed eyes and perfect feminine grooming, despite her masculine attire and tough, aggressive behavior. The *New York Times* chose to ridicule both DeMille's distortion of history and Arthur's "cute" and "tomboyish" characterization. However, *Photoplay* magazine's reviewer gave the actress more respect: "Jean Arthur, as the famous frontier woman, handles the role superbly, keeping the rough and ready character appealingly sympathetic."

### History is Made at Night

(United Artists: 1937) 97 minutes.

Director: Frank Borzage. Producer: Walter Wanger. Screenplay: Gene Towne, Graham Baker, and (uncredited) Joshua Logan and Arthur Ripley. Additional Dialogue: Vincent Lawrence and David Hertz. Based on the book *Personal History* by Vincent Sheehan. Cinematographer: David Abel and (uncredited) Gregg Toland. Special Effects: James Basevi. Editor: Margaret Clancey. Art Director: Alexander Toluboff. Costumes: Bernard Newman. Musical Director: Alfred Newman. Sound: Paul Neal. Assistant Director: Lew Borzage.

*Cast:* Charles Boyer (*Paul Dumond*); Jean Arthur (*Irene Vail*); Leo Carrillo (*Cesare*); Colin Clive (*Bruce Vail*); Ivan Lebedeff (*Michael*); George Meeker (*Norton*); Lucien Prival (*Detective Witness*); George Renavent (*Inspector Millard*); George Davies (*Maestro*); Adele St. Mauer (*Hotel Maid*); Byron Foulger (*Secretary*); Pierre Watkin (*Commodore*); George Humbert (*Ship's Chef*); Senor Wences (*Specialty Performer*); Jack Mulhall (*Waiter*); Robert Parrish (*Ship's Passenger*).

*The Film:* Loaned out to Walter Wanger Productions, Jean Arthur was elegantly costumed by favored designer Bernard Newman in this incredible mixture of farce and tragedy opposite the French-born screen idol Charles Boyer. Here, she's the unhappy wife of insanely jealous shipbuilder Colin Clive, who makes her life miserable

Ivan Lebedeff, Charles Boyer and JA in *History Is Made at Night* (United Artists, 1937).

127

when she seeks a divorce. Plot complications then involve her with Boyer, an urbane headwaiter who pretends to be a jewel thief, and with whom she eventually falls in love. Ultimately, the husband's suicide paves the way for the protagonists' future happiness.

Seriously challenged by the mood-shifting narrative, director Frank Borzage somehow managed to make the screenplay's disparate elements work, with Boyer and Arthur well teamed at underplaying the melodramatic twists and turns. For Arthur, her role held darker elements than any of her previous movies, and in that light her work here is quite extraordinary. Reflecting a deep-set inner sadness, her character finds a consistency of tone that almost makes the storyline credible, against all odds.

Understandably, *Variety*'s critic said, "It's hard to believe this one for a minute," before allowing that it was a "mildly entertaining picture with good names." The *New York Times* held similar views, conceding that only its cast made the film enjoyable. *Screen Book* magazine was more optimistic: "Melodrama, comedy, romance—these three elements in combination with striking performances by Charles Boyer and Jean Arthur assure a smashing box-office success."

### *Easy Living*

(Paramount; 1937) 86 minutes.
Director: Mitchell Leisen. Producer: Arthur Hornblow Jr. Screenplay: Preston Sturges. Based on an unpublished story by Vera Caspary. Cinematographer: Ted Tetzlaff. Special Effects: Farciot Edouart. Editor: Doane Harrison. Art Directors: Hans Dreier and Ernst Fegté. Set Decorator: A. E. Freudeman. Costumes: Travis Banton. Music Director: Boris Morros. Sound: Earl Hayman and William Thayer.

*Cast*: Jean Arthur (*Mary Smith*); Edward Arnold (*J. B. Ball*); Ray Milland (*John Ball Jr.*); Luis Alberni (*Mr. Louis Louis*); Mary Nash (*Mrs. Ball*); Franklin Pangborn (*Van Buren*); Barlowe Borland (*Mr. Gurney*);William Demarest (*Wallace Whistling*); Andrew Tombes (*E. F. Hulgar*); Esther Dale (*Lillian*); Harlan Briggs (*Office Manager*);William B. Davidson (*Mr. Hyde*); Nora Cecil (*Miss Swerf*); Robert Greig (*Butler*); Bennie Bartlett (*Newsboy*); Florence Dudley (*Cashier*); Gertrude Astor

Ray Milland and JA in Easy Living
(Paramount Pictures, 1937).

(*Saleswoman*); Bud Flanagan/Dennis O'Keefe (*Office Manager*); Stanley Andrews (*Captain*).

*The Film*: The third and last of Jean Arthur's 1937 loan-out releases returned her to Paramount for this Cinderella fable, based by screenwriter Preston Sturges on a Vera Caspary story. *Easy Living* casts her as a Manhattan stenographer, riding atop a Fifth Avenue bus, who gets the fur coat dropped from a window by exasperated tycoon Edward Arnold. When she returns it, she's unexpectedly installed in a posh hotel suite and mistakenly believed to be Arnold's mistress. Consequently, she loses her job and gets involved with his wayward son (Ray Milland), a busboy at the Automat—all in whimsical, screwball fashion. Rife with breezy misunderstandings, the plot dances madly on, elaborating on its one-joke premise as Arthur and Milland fall in love. But their romance is complicated by her innocent friendship with benefactor Arnold, until everything is patched up in time to reach a Depression-era fairy-tale ending.

Under the inspired, sometimes experimental direction of Mitchell Leisen (*Hands Across the Table*), *Easy Living* was well enough received in 1937, though not considered anything out of the ordinary. Leisen encouraged Jean Arthur to underplay her character, while those about her appear to have pulled out all farcical stops in the old Mack Sennett tradition. *Variety* reported, "Miss Arthur is attractive and does her best with an impossible part." *Modern Screen*'s astute reviewer was more readily impressed: "This is Miss Arthur's finest performance, and she's given ample opportunity to demonstrate her delightful flair for light comedy." Allowing that *Easy Living* "has its merits," the *New York Times* singled out Arthur and Arnold "who have the gift of understanding farce—if that be possible." In more recent years, this picture has become a favorite of classic-film buffs, with its beautifully timed performances and hilarious comic inventions.

### You Can't Take It With You

(Columbia; 1938) 127 minutes.
Director/Producer: Frank Capra. Screenplay: Robert Riskin. Based on the play by George S. Kaufman and Moss Hart. Cinematographer: Joseph Walker. Editor: Gene Havlick. Art Directors: Stephen Goosson and Lionel Banks. Costumes: Bernard Newman and Irene. Music Score: Dmitri Tiomkin. Music Director: Morris Stoloff. Sound: John Livadary.
*Cast*: Jean Arthur (*Alice Sycamore*); Lionel Barrymore (*Martin Vanderhof*);

JA, Spring Byington and Lionel Barrymore in You Can't Take It With You (Columbia Pictures, 1938).

James Stewart (*Tony Kirby*); Edward Arnold (*Anthony P. Kirby*); Mischa Auer *(Kolenkhov)*; Ann Miller (*Essie Carmichael*); Spring Byington (*Penny Sycamore*); Donald Meek (*Poppins*); H. B. Warner (*Ramsey*); Halliwell Hobbes (*De Pinna*); Dub Taylor (*Ed Carmichael*); Mary Forbes (*Mrs. Anthony Kirby*); Lillian Yarbo (*Rheba*); Eddie Anderson (*Donald*); Clarence Wilson (*John Blakely*); Joseph Swickard (*Professor*); Ann Doran (*Maggie O'Neill*); Christian Rub (*Schmidt*); Bodil Rosing (*Mrs. Schmidt*); Charles Lane (*Henderson*); Harry Davenport (*Judge*); Pierre Watkin, Edwin Maxwell and Russell Hicks (*Attorneys*); Byron Foulger (*Kirby's Assistant*); James Flavin (*Jailer*); Ian Wolfe (*Kirby's Secretary*); Irving Bacon (*Henry*); Chester Clute (*Hammond*); Pert Kelton and Kit Guard (*Jail Inmates*); James Burke and Ward Bond (*Detectives*); Robert Greig (*Lord Melville*); Dick Curtis (*Strong-arm Man*).

*The Film:* The Kaufman and Hart comedy hit of the 1936-37 Broadway season had won a Pulitzer Prize, and was therefore considered a sure bet for Hollywood. But, rather than play it safe by adhering closely to the whacky, slapstick original, producer-director Frank Capra encouraged ace screenwriter Robert Riskin to "open it up" and considerably re-tailor it for the movies, while also adding warmth and genuine sentiment (versus sentimentality) to the interrelationships. Riskin also managed to make the play's inherent humor thought-provoking.

Arthur plays the independent daughter of an eccentric, uninhibited family who falls for her wealthy, conventional boss (James Stewart)—to the dismay of his snobbish mother (Mary Forbes) and tycoon father (Edward Arnold). Things come to a head when Stewart and his family are invited to dinner and arrive a day early, for chaos immediately ensues. The plot enjoys some added twists before the typical Capra-esque ending in which everyone mends their ways and begins to appreciate one another.

At 37, Jean Arthur was still able to channel the child in her psyche that enabled her to remain convincing while sliding down a banister or reacting to imaginary mice with screams in a busy restaurant. The *New York Times* found the movie's characters "far more likable, far more human" than in the stage play, and termed it "a grand picture." *Variety*'s critic wrote: "Miss Arthur, the very appealing quality of her speaking voice carrying her far on the screen and again here, acquits herself creditably."

*You Can't Take It With You* was among the 1938-39 season's top grossing films, and won Frank Capra his third Best Director Oscar, as well as garnering him a companion statuette as producer of 1938's Best Picture.

## Only Angels Have Wings
(Columbia; 1939) 121 minutes.
Director/Producer: Howard Hawks. Screenplay: Jules Furthman and (uncredited) William Rankin and Eleanor Griffin. Story: Howard Hawks.

Cinematographers: Joseph Walker and Elmer Dyer. Special Effects: Roy Davidson and Edwin C. Hallor. Editor: Viola Lawrence. Art Director: Lionel Banks. Costumes: Kalloch. Music: Dmitri Tiomkin. Music Director: Morris Stoloff. Technical Advisor: Paul Mantz. Assistant Director: Arthur S. Black.

*Cast*: Cary Grant (*Geoff Carter*); Jean Arthur (*Bonnie Lee*); Richard Barthelmess (*Bat McPherson*); Rita Hayworth (*Judy McPherson*); Thomas Mitchell (*Kid Dabb*); Allyn Joslyn (*Les Peters*); Sig Ruman (*Dutchman*); Victor Kilian (*Sparks*); John Carroll (*Gent Shelton*); Donald Barry (*Tex Gordon*); Noah Beery Jr. (*Joe Souther*); Manuel Magiste (*Balladeer*); Milissa Sierra (*Lily*); Pat Flaherty (*Mike*); Pedro Regas (*Pancho*); Pat West (*Baldy*); Lucio Villegas (*Dr. Logario*); Forbes Murray (*Hartwood*); Sammee Tong (*Native*); Candy Candido (*Musician*); Charles Moore (*Servant*); Inez Palange (*Lily's Aunt*); Rafael Corio (*Purser*).

*The Film*: Howard Hawks produced and directed this characteristically well-made melodrama about personality clashes and romantic complications among mail pilots in Central America. Jean Arthur plays a stranded Brooklyn showgirl who falls for freedom-loving chief flyer Cary Grant, whose life is complicated further by the appearance of ex-flame Rita Hayworth, now married to a new arrival, pilot Richard Barthelmess. Old enmities soon surface, in addition to dangerously challenging weather conditions, to heighten the typically Hawksian dramatics.

The *New York Times* reflected the critical consensus when they opined, " . . . a less convincing showgirl than Miss Arthur would be hard to find." However, the actress enacts her part with dedicated sincerity, and even plays the piano for a brief musical interlude in an early scene. Nowhere is there an indication of her differences with producer-director Hawks, her objections to co-star Grant's on-the-set behavior or her prevalent jealousy of sexy ingénue Hayworth. All told, this was not a happy filming experience for Arthur.

Thomas Mitchell, Sig Rumann, JA and Cary Grant in Only Angels Have Wings (Columbia Pictures, 1939).

*Jerry Vermilye*

## Mr. Smith Goes To Washington

(Columbia; 1939) 129 minutes.

Director/Producer: Frank Capra. Screenplay: Sidney Buchman. Based on the story "The Gentleman from Montana" by Lewis R. Foster. Cinematographer: Joseph Walker. Editors: Gene Havlick and Al Clark. Art Director: Lionel Banks. Montage Effects: Slavko Vorkapich. Costumes: Kalloch. Music: Dmitri Tiomkin. Music Director: Morris Stoloff. Sound: John Livadary. Assistant Director: Arthur S. Black.

*Cast*: Jean Arthur (*Clarissa Saunders*); James Stewart (*Jefferson Smith*); Claude Rains (*Sen. Joseph Paine*); Edward Arnold (*Jim Taylor*); Guy Kibbee (*Gov. Hubert Hopper*); Thomas Mitchell (*Diz Moore*); Eugene Pallette (*Chick McGann*); Beulah Bondi (*Ma Smith*); H. B. Warner (*Senator Fuller*); Harry Carey (*President of the Senate*); Astrid Allwyn (*Susan Paine*); Ruth Donnelly (*Mrs. Hopper*); Grant Mitchell (*Senator McPherson*); Porter Hall (*Senator Monroe*); H. V. Kaltenborn (*Broadcaster*); Pierre Watkin (*Senator Barnes*); Charles Lane (*Nosey*); William Demarest (*Biff Griffith*); Dick Elliott (*Carl Cook*); Larry Simms, Billy Watson, Delmar Watson, Harry Watson, Garry Watson and John Russell (*The Hopper Boys*); Jack Carson (*Sweeney*); Maurice Costello (*Diggs*); Byron Foulger (*Hopper's Secretary*); Frances Gifford, Linda Winters/Dorothy Comingore, Adrian Booth (*Girls*); Fred "Snowflake" Toones and Charles Moore (*Porters*); Mary Gordon and June Gittelson (*Women*); Russell Simpson (*Ken Allen*); Ann Doran and Helen Jerome Eddy (*Paine's Secretaries*); Vera Lewis (*Mrs. Edwards*); Gino Corrado (*Barber*); George Chandler, Evalyn Knapp, Dub Taylor and Eddie Kane (*Reporters*).

*The Film*: Jean Arthur's last film with Frank Capra was this classic blend of comedy and drama, amusingly naïve heroes and corrupt, power-hungry villains. Capra's personal commitment to flag-waving commentary on American idealism and political chicanery centers on a trio of movies, commencing with 1936's *Mr. Deeds Goes to Town* and ending with 1941's *Meet John Doe*. Best of the lot is the brilliant centerpiece, for *Mr. Smith Goes to Washington* is a triumphant amalgam of script, director and truly inspired performances.

JA, James Stewart and Thomas Mitchell in Mr. Smith Goes to Washington (Columbia Pictures, 1939).

The nation's capital provides the locale for Sidney Buchman's

132

well-wrought screenplay about a green, Wisconsin senator (James Stewart) who learns the hard way about Washington graft and corruption, which he idealistically discloses in a memorable climactic speech before the Senate.

In a fine cast, Claude Rains offers a masterful display of corruption battling conscience, and Arthur alternates endearingly between warm support and tart cynicism as the all-wise Girl Friday who helps Stewart beat those governmental odds. *Variety* called her performance "excellent," and the *New York Times* observed, "Jean Arthur as the secretary tosses a line and bats an eye with delightful drollery."

It's well known that 1939 was a unique year of great moviemaking and, although it received an impressive 11 Academy Award nominations, *Mr. Smith Goes to Washington*'s only win was Lewis R. Foster for Best Original Story. An updated 1977 remake called *Billy Jack Goes to Washington* did nothing to replace memories of the 1939 original.

### Too Many Husbands

(Columbia; 1940) 84 minutes.

Director/Producer: Wesley Ruggles. Screenplay: Claude Binyon. Based on the play *Home and Beauty* by W. Somerset Maugham. Cinematographer: Joseph Walker. Editors: Otto Meyer and William Lyon. Art Director: Lionel Banks. Music: Frederick Hollander. Music Director: Morris Stoloff. Assistant Director: Arthur S. Black.

*Cast*: Jean Arthur (*Vicky Lowndes*); Fred MacMurray (*Bill Cardew*); Melvyn Douglas (*Henry Lowndes*); Harry Davenport (*George*); Dorothy Peterson (*Gertrude Houlihan*); Melville Cooper (*Peter*); Edgar Buchanan (*McDermott*); Tom Dugan (*Sullivan*); Garry Owen (*Sign Painter*); Lee "Lasses" White (*Mailman*); Mary Treen (*Emma*); William Brisbane (*Lawyer*); Sam McDaniel (*Porter*); Ralph Peters (*Cab Driver*); Walter Soderling (*Customer*); Jerry Fletcher (*Man*); Jacques Vanaire (*Headwaiter*).

*The Film*: In a year that saw the release of two movies with the same Enoch Arden theme, *Too Many Husbands* emerged the weaker contender next to RKO's more successful *My Favorite Wife*. The latter finds "widower" Cary Grant marrying Gail Patrick, unaware that his presumed-drowned first wife, Irene Dunne, is not only alive

JA, Fred MacMurray, Harry Davenport and Melvyn Douglas in Too Many Husbands (Columbia Pictures, 1940).

but eager to resume their marital relationship. And the audience is left with little doubt that the original pair will somehow get back together. The situation is reversed in *Too Many Husbands*, wherein Fred MacMurray's the "late" husband who returns to find wife Jean Arthur already remarried, to his friend Melvyn Douglas! Which husband will she choose? Neither of them is given any admirable qualities with which the audience can identify, although Arthur appears equally to enjoy the company of both. Despite the fact that different endings were shot, leaving Arthur with first MacMurray and then Douglas, the release version concludes with a stalemate, implying that all three will continue as a *ménage à trois.*

Basically, an expert cast is wasted in this pleasantly diverting little comedy of errors that could have used more help from both screenwriter Claude Binyon and producer-director Wesley Ruggles. *Variety*'s benevolent critic wrote: "Jean Arthur, Fred MacMurray and Melvyn Douglas . . . romp through this in a delightful way that is apt to leave you gasping for breath in the aisle."

In 1955, Columbia filmed a musical remake under the title *Three for the Show* that made little impression on anyone.

### *Arizona*

(Columbia; 1940) 127 minutes.

Director/Producer: Wesley Ruggles. Screenplay: Claude Binyon. Based on the novel by Clarence Budington Kelland. Cinematographers: Joseph Walker (Interiors), Harry Hallenberger and Fayte Brown (Exteriors). Editors: Otto Meyer and William Lyon. Art Directors: Lionel Banks and Robert Peterson. Set Decoration: Frank Tuttle. Costumes: Kalloch. Sound: George Cooper. Music: Victor Young. Musical Direction: Morris Stoloff. Technical Advisor: Chief Fighting Bear. Assistant Director: Norman Deming.

As Phoebe Titus in Arizona (Columbia Pictures, 1940).

*Cast:* Jean Arthur (*Phoebe Titus*); William Holden (*Peter Muncie*); Warren William (*Jefferson Carteret*); Porter Hall (*Lazarus Ward*); Edgar Buchanan (*Judge Bogardus*); Paul Harvey (*Solomon Warner*); George Chandler (*Haley*) Byron Foulger (*Pete Kitchen*); Regis Toomey (*Grant Oury*); Paul Lopez (*Estavan Ochoa*); Colin Tapley (*Bart Massey*); Uvaldo Varela (*Hilario Gallego*); Earl Crawford (*Joe Briggs*); Griff Barnette (*Sam Hughes*); Ludwig Hardt (*Meyer*); Patrick

Moriarty (*Terry*); Frank Darien (*Joe*); Syd Saylor (*Timmins*); Wade Crosby (*Longstreet*); Frank Hill (*Mano*); Nina Campana (*Teresa*); Addison Richards (*Captain Hunter*); Kermit Maynard (*Bill Oury*); Earle S. Dewey (*Bill Coombs*); Jerry Fletcher (*Harry Coombs*); Ralph Peters (*Bartender*); Emmett Lynn (*Leatherface*); Walter Baldwin (*Man Who Declares for South*); William Harrigan (*Union Commanding Officer*).

*The Film*: Most of *Arizona* was shot on Tucson area locations in the spring and early summer of 1940, where temperatures sometimes reached 130 degrees. Thus, it wasn't an easy production for either cast or crew. Arthur had an arrangement with producer-director Wesley Ruggles (*Too Many Husbands*) that allowed her to start work an hour earlier than other cast members, and then enjoy an extended two-hour lunch break, thus allowing her to shower, eat and nap for an hour before the afternoon resumption of filming. For this production, a small pre-Civil War village was built in the desert 17 miles south of Tucson. It would later be utilized for many Western productions (i.e., *Gunfight at the O.K. Corral*), and become a major tourist attraction known as "Old Tucson."

*Arizona*'s sprawling Claude Binyon screenplay set just before the War Between the States, teams rugged pie-stand operator Arthur opposite restless drifter William Holden, who arrives in town and starts courting her. Arthur moves into the freighting business, hoping that Holden will work in her employ. But he departs for California, suggesting he'll return for her. Meanwhile, she finds herself up against town crook Porter Hall, who secretly joins forces with conniving Tucson newcomer Warren William. Holden returns to wed Arthur, but first she sends him off to Montana to buy cattle. The rest of this episodic yarn involves the villains sponsoring an Indian attack, the arrival of the cattle and a gun battle that ends in favor of the protagonists.

Although the creative minds of Ruggles and Binyon must have had Jean Arthur's Calamity Jane performance in mind when they conceived *Arizona*'s Phoebe Titus, the latter character lacks both the underlying femininity and subtleties of *The Plainsman*. While never dull, *Arizona* fails to attain the audience-grabbing showmanship Cecil B. DeMille knew so much about. However, Arthur garnered some of the movie's best notices. *Variety* reported: "Jean Arthur dominates throughout with her strongly convincing performance of a pioneer girl, shading character believably from hardness in dealing with men to softness for romance with Holden." *Silver Screen*'s reviewer wrote, "Jean gives a grand performance as the tough, mannish Phoebe." And *Photoplay/Movie Mirror* recklessly pulled out all the stops: "Jean Arthur as Phoebe surpasses anything she has yet done and proves herself one of the top actresses of the screen."

## The Devil and Miss Jones

(RKO; 1941) 92 minutes.

Director: Sam Wood. Producer: Frank Ross. Screenplay: Norman Krasna. Cinematographer: Harry Stradling. Editor: Sherman Todd. Production Designer: William Cameron Menzies. Art Director: Van Nest Polglase. Special Effects: Vernon L. Walker and Albert S. D'Agostino. Costumes: Irene. Music Direction: Roy Webb. Sound: John L. Cass.

Cast: Jean Arthur (*Mary Jones*); Robert Cummings (*Joe O'Brien*); Charles Coburn (*John P. Merrick*); Edmund Gwenn (*Hooper*); Spring Byington (*Elizabeth Ellis*); S. Z. Sakall (*George*); William Demarest (*First Detective*); Walter Kingsford (*Allison*); Montagu Love (*Harrison*); Richard Carle (*Oliver*); Charles Waldron (*Needles*); Edwin Maxwell (*Withers*); Edward McNamara (*Police Sergeant*); Robert Emmett Keane (*Thomas Higgins*); Florence Bates (*Shoe Customer*); Charles Irwin (*Second Detective*); Matt McHugh (*Sam*); Julie Warren (*Dorothy*); Ilene Brewer (*Sally*); Regis Toomey (*First Policeman*); Pat Moriarty (*Second Policeman*).

*The Film*: Although tailored for Jean Arthur by her producer-husband Frank Ross, in collaboration with screenwriter Norman Krasna, *The Devil and Miss Jones* is really more of a showcase for the wonderful character actor Charles Coburn, who understandably steals the show. Arthur plays a salesgirl in a large department store who helps new employee Coburn, never suspecting that he's their much-hated boss, whose business tactics have inspired his workers to try to unionize. Predictably, Coburn changes from cold-hearted millionaire to benevolent convert, and takes a romantic interest in saleswoman Spring Byington.

Arthur's character has her own subsidiary romance with Robert Cummings, but it's interesting to note the generosity with which she and Frank Ross defer

Charles Coburn and JA in The Devil and Miss Jones (RKO Radio Pictures, 1941).

to third-billed Coburn for the story's main focus. And, in contrast to *Easy Living*'s scatterbrained Mary Smith, *Devil*'s Mary *Jones* is quite levelheaded while nevertheless amusing in her comedy scenes, delivered in a straightforward, non-cutesy style under Sam Wood's direction.

In *Movie-Radio Guide*, Carl A. Schroeder praised the movie's unexpected shift in focus: "A fine thing about *The Devil and Miss Jones* is that Jean Arthur isn't in every foot of the opus, giving out with that startled look that is so cute when it isn't overdone." The *New York Times* lauded both the film and its sterling cast: "All are good, all contribute to a picture which is delightfully piquant."

### The Talk of the Town

(Columbia; 1942) 118 minutes.

Director/Producer: George Stevens. Associate Producer: Fred Guiol. Screenplay: Irwin Shaw and Sidney Buchman. Adaptation: Dale Van Every. Based on the story by Sidney Harmon. Cinematographer: Ted Tetzlaff. Editor: Otto Meyer. Art Direction: Lionel Banks and Rudolph Sternad. Montage Effects: Donald Starling. Costumes: Irene. Sound: Lodge Cunningham. Music: Frederick Hollander. Music Director: Morris Stoloff. Assistant Director: Norman Deming.

*Cast:* Cary Grant (*Leopold Dilg*); Jean Arthur (*Nora Shelley*); Ronald Colman (*Michael Lightcap*); Edgar Buchanan (*Sam Yates*); Glenda Farrell (*Regina Bush*); Charles Dingle (*Andrew Holmes*); Emma Dunn (*Mrs. Shelley*); Rex Ingram (*Tilney*); Leonid Kinskey (*Jan Pulaski*); Tom Tyler (*Clyde Bracken*); Don Beddoe (*Chief of Police*); George Watts (*Judge Grunstadt*); Clyde Fillmore (*Sen. James Boyd*); Frank M. Thomas (*District Attorney*); Lloyd Bridges (*Forrester*); Pat McVey (*Cop*); Eddie Laughton (*Henry*); Billy Benedict (*Western Union Boy*); Ferike Boros (*Mrs. Pulaski*); Lee "Lasses" White (*Hound Keeper*); Dewey Robinson (*Jake*); Lew Davis and Gino Corrado (*Waiters*); Frank Sully (*Road Cop*); Dan Seymour (*Headwaiter*); Mabel Todd (*Operator*); Clarence Muse (*Doorkeeper*); Leslie Brooks (*Secretary*); Robert Walker (*Deputy Sheriff*).

Cary Grant and JA in The Talk of the Town (Columbia Pictures, 1942).

*The Film:* The first of several pictures producer-director George Stevens was signed to turn out for Columbia was this unusual mixture of whacky comedy and social conscience, reminiscent of Frank Capra. Arthur plays a schoolmarm who gets law professor Ronald Colman to defend fugitive radical Cary Grant. After his acquittal, she winds up with the professor.

Among the film's champions was the *New York Times*' Bosley Crowther: "*The Talk of the Town* is going to make a lot of people laugh and feel good. It may be off-beam in its philosophy, but its quality of humor is not strained." And he added, "Miss Arthur is charming, as usual, in her bewilderment." *Variety*'s critic concurred: "Miss Arthur adds another clear-cut comedy characterization as the schoolteacher." *Photoplay* placed Arthur's Nora Shelley among the month's best performances, concluding "Miss Arthur is always delightful."

### The More the Merrier

(Columbia; 1943) 104 minutes.

Director/Producer: George Stevens. Associate Producer: Fred Guiol. Screenplay: Robert Russell, Frank Ross, Richard Flournoy and Lewis R. Foster. Story: Robert Russell and Frank Ross. Cinematographer: Ted Tetzlaff. Editor: Otto Meyer. Art Direction: Lionel Banks and Rudolph Sternad. Interior Decoration: Fay Babcock. Music: Leigh Harline. "The Torpedo Song" by Henry Myers, Edward Eliscu and Jay Gorney. Music Direction: Morris Stoloff. Assistant Director: Norman Deming.

*Cast:* Jean Arthur (*Connie Milligan*); Joel McCrea (*Joe Carter*); Charles Coburn (*Benjamin Dingle*); Richard Gaines (*Charles J. Pendergast*); Bruce Bennett (*Evans*); Frank Sully (*Pike*); Don Douglas (*Harding*); Clyde Fillmore (*Senator Noonan*); Stanley Clements (*Morton Rodakiewicz*); Grady Sutton (*Waiter*); Ann Savage (*Miss Dalton*); Sugar Geise (*Dancer*); Don Barclay (*Drunk*); Ann Doran (*Miss Bilby*); Mary Treen (*Waitress*); Gladys Burke (*Barmaid*); Kay Linaker (*Miss Allen*); Nancy Gay (*Miss Chasen*); Byron Shores (*Air Corps Captain*); Betzi Beaton (*Miss Finch*); Harrison Greene (*Texan*); Robert McKenzie (*Southerner*); Vic Potel (*Cattleman*); Harry Bradley (*Minister*); Betty McMahon (*Miss Greskin*); Chester Clute (*Hotel Clerk*).

*The Film*: In a nutshell, *The More the Merrier* is set in overcrowded World War II Washington, where philanthropist Charles Coburn plays cupid to landlady Jean Arthur and fellow-lodger Joel McCrea amid the housing shortage. Reunited with her most recent director, George Stevens, as well as congenial previous co-stars Coburn and McCrea, Arthur has here a tailor-made role in which she absolutely shines. Especially delightful are the early scenes she performs so amusingly with Coburn. He's moved in to share

JA, Charles Coburn and Joel McCrea in *The More the Merrier* (Columbia Pictures, 1943).

her spacious apartment, and she reads him her carefully-thought-out plan for their morning schedule. All this is handled with deadly seriousness as she delivers the long list of activities almost in a single breath. In fact, this introductory section of the movie is so humorously perfect that the remainder of *The More the Merrier*, good though it is, can only suffer by comparison. Nevertheless, this is one of the best comedies of the Forties, and it garnered well deserved Academy Award nominations for Best Actress Arthur (her *only* nomination) and Best Supporting Actor Coburn. Coburn won, but his teammate lost to *The Song of Bernadette*'s little-known Jennifer Jones. Small compensation perhaps, but *Variety* opined: "Miss Arthur makes the most out of what is undoubtedly the best screen role of her long Hollywood career."

Joel McCrea and JA in *The More the Merrier*
(Columbia Pictures, 1943).

### A Lady Takes a Chance

(RKO; 1943) 86 minutes.
Director: William A. Seiter. Producer: Frank Ross. Associate Producer: Richard Ross. Screenplay: Robert Ardrey. Original Story: Jo Swerling. Cinematographer: Frank Redman. Special Effects: Vernon L. Walker. Editor: Theron Warth. Art Directors: Albert S. D'Agostino and Alfred Herman. Set Decorators: Darrell Silvera and Al Fields. Costumes: Edward Stevenson. Music: Roy Webb. Music Director: C. Bakaleinikoff.

John Wayne and JA in A Lady Takes a Chance (RKO Radio Pictures, 1943).

139

Sound: Roy Meadows and James G. Stewart. Assistant Director: J. D. Starkey.

*Cast:* Jean Arthur (*Mollie Truesdale*); John Wayne (*Duke Hudk*ins); Charles Winninger (*Waco*); Phil Silvers (*Smiley Lambert*); Mary Field (*Florrie Bendix*); Don Costello (*Drunk*); John Philliber (*Storekeeper*); Grady Sutton (*Malcolm Stocky*); Grant Withers (*Bob Hastings*); Hans Conreid (*Greg Stone*); Peggy Carroll (*Jitterbug*); Ariel Heath (*Flossie*); Sugar Geise (*Linda Belle*); Joan Blair (*Lilly*); Tom Fadden (*Mullen*); Cy Kendall (*Saloon Owner*); Alex Melesh (*Bartender*); Charles D. Brown (*Dr. Humboldt*); Nena Quartaro (*Carmencita*); Ralf Harolde (*Croupier*); Dorothy Granger (*Hot Dog Girl*); Lane Chandler (*Slim*); Harry Semels (*Greek*).

*The Film:* Frank Ross was the full-fledged producer of this Western comedy, in association with his brother Richard. It would be their last such collaboration on a Jean Arthur movie. In her only teaming with soon-to-be-superstar John Wayne, she's an Easterner who becomes involved with a cowboy during a vacation bus tour of the West. Eventually, she lands him, but on *her* terms. The two stars played well together, handling their comedy scenes with ease under the uninspired direction of William A. Seiter. Even such reliable members of the supporting cast as Charles Winninger, Phil Silvers and Mary Field seem more subdued than usual, as though Seiter (or perhaps producer Ross?) were afraid they might steal scenes from Wayne and Arthur.

*Variety*'s supportive critic said, "*Lady* gives Jean Arthur one of her best roles," and called it "a highly entertaining romantic comedy." In the *New York Times*, Theodore Strauss wrote her a Valentine: "If *A Lady Takes a Chance* is quite continuously amusing, it is largely because of Miss Arthur's pert little ways, her prim hesitations at the wrong times, her uncloying coyness. Quite gradually, she has become one of Hollywood's delightful comediennes."

## The Impatient Years

(Columbia; 1944) 91 minutes.

Director/Producer: Irving Cummings. Screenplay: Virginia Van Upp. Cinematographers: Joseph Walker and Burnett Guffey. Editor: Al Clark. Assistant Director: Abby Berlin. Art Directors: Lionel Banks and Cary Odell. Set Decorator: Ross Dowd. Costumes: Jean Louis. Sound: Ed Bernds. Song: "Who Said Dreams Don't Come True?" by Harry Akst, Benny Davis and Al Jolson.

*Cast:* Jean Arthur (*Janie Anderson*); Lee Bowman (*Andy Anderson*); Charles Coburn (*William Smith*); Edgar Buchanan (*Judge*); Charley Grapewin (*Bellboy*); Phil Brown (*Henry Fairchild*); Harry Davenport (*Minister*); Jane Darwell (*Minister's Wife*); Grant Mitchell (*Hotel Clerk*); Frank Jenks (*Top Sergeant*); Frank Orth (*Counterman*); Charles Arnt (*Marriage License*

*Clerk*); Robert Emmett Keane (*Attorney*); Vic Beaver (*Baby*); Regina Wallace (*Nurse*).

*The Film*: In her final contracted picture for Columbia, 43-year-old Jean Arthur co-starred with 29-year-old Lee Bowman (a second-rate replacement for the originally set Joel McCrea) in the minimally amusing story of a soldier, his war bride and their adjustment problems following his return from overseas. There was nothing inspired about this project, and even the presence of an expert supporting cast (Charles Coburn, Edgar Buchanan, Harry Davenport, Jane Darwell, et al) couldn't make it anything special.

Critical reviews were mildly polite, although the *New York Times*' Bosley Crowther labeled the comedy "meager." Jean Arthur's best personal notice came from *Photoplay* magazine, which called her "still the best farceur in the business." For whatever reasons, it would be nearly four years before Arthur's return to the screen.

## A Foreign Affair

(Paramount; 1948) 116 minutes.

Director: Billy Wilder. Producer: Charles Brackett. Screenplay: Charles Brackett, Billy Wilder and Richard Breen. Adaptation: Robert Harari. Original Story: David Shaw and Irwin Shaw. Cinematographer: Charles Lang Jr. Special Effects: Gordon Jennings. Process Photography: Farciot Edouart and Dewey Wrigley. Editor: Doane Harrison. Art Directors: Hans Dreier and Walter Tyler. Set Decorators: Sam Comer and Ross Dowd. Costumes: Edith Head. Sound: Hugo Grenzbach and Walter Oberst. Music: Frederick Hollander, incl. Marlene Dietrich's songs "Black Market," "Illusions" and "Ruins of Berlin." Assistant Director: C. C. Coleman Jr.

*Cast:* Jean Arthur (*Phoebe Frost*); Marlene Dietrich (*Erika von Schluetow*); John Lund (*Capt. John Pringle*); Millard Mitchell (*Col. Rufus J. Plummer*); Peter Von Zerneck (*Hans Otto Birgel*); Stanley Prager (*Mike*); Bill Murphy (*Joe*); Gordon Jones (*First M. P.*); Freddie Steele (*Second M. P.*); Raymond Bond (*Pennecott*);Boyd Davis (*Griffin*); Robert Malcolm (*Kraus*); Charles Meredith (*Yandell*); Michael Raffetto (*Salvatore*); James Larmore (*Lieutenant Hornby*); Damien O'Flynn (*Lieutenant Colonel*); Frederick Hollander (*Pianist*); Frank Fenton (*Major Matthews*); Bobby Watson (*Adolf Hitler in film clip*); Henry Kulky (*Russian Sergeant*); Harland Tucker (*General McAndrew*); George Carleton (*General Finney*); Edward Van Sloan (*German Man*); Lisa Golm (*German Woman*); Ilka Gruning (*German Wife*); Paul Panzer (*German Husband*).

*The Film*: After turning down Hollywood offers for leading roles in such major productions as *Anna and the King of Siam, It's a Wonderful Life, The Voice of the Turtle* and *The Bishop's Wife*, Jean Arthur finally elected to return to the screen for director Billy Wilder in *A Foreign Affair*. It's set

JA, John Lund and Marlene Dietrich in A Foreign Affair (Paramount Pictures, 1948).

in postwar Berlin, where a Congressional committee arrives to inspect GI morale and conditions. Arthur plays a prim member of the group who takes exception to the behavior she observes involving American soldiers consorting with German women. Her main target becomes café singer Marlene Dietrich, and she seeks the help of Army captain John Lund, never dreaming he's the man with whom Dietrich's associated. Charmed by Lund, Arthur softens and, in one amusing nightclub sequence, she becomes intoxicated and breaks out in "The Iowa Corn Song." Since she and Lund both hail from Iowa, they share common origins, and he romances her to distract her from Dietrich. Plot complications temporarily keep this romantic triangle alive until, finally, Arthur gets her man.

Even when prettied up in an evening dress, 47-year-old Arthur presents a dowdy contrast to Dietrich, whose glamour still held fast at 46. And so it's difficult to accept a Lund-Arthur alliance at the movie's fadeout. The *New York Times* review called Arthur "beautifully droll," while *Variety* extended its welcome: "Jean Arthur is back in a topflight characterization after a considerable screen absence."

### Shane

(Paramount; 1953) 118 minutes. Director/Producer: George Stevens. Associate Producer: Ivan Moffat. Screenplay: A. B. Guthrie Jr. and Jack Sher. Based on the novel by Jack Schaefer. Technicolor Cinematographer: Loyal Griggs. Second-Unit Photography: Irmin Roberts. Process Photography: Farciot Edouart. Special Effects: Gordon Jennings. Editors: William Hornbeck and Tom McAdoo. Art Direction: Hal Pereira and Walter

Alan Ladd, Van Heflin, JA and Brandon De Wilde in Shane (Paramount Pictures, 1953).

142

Tyler. Set Decoration: Emile Kuri. Costumes: Edith Head. Sound: Harry Lindgren and Gene Garvin. Music: Victor Young. Technical Advisor: Joe DeYong. Assistant Director: John Coonan.

*Cast:* Alan Ladd (*Shane*); Jean Arthur (*Marian Starrett*); Van Heflin (*Joe Starrett*); Brandon De Wilde (*Joey Starrett*); Walter [Jack] Palance (*Jack Wilson*); Ben Johnson (*Chris Callaway*); Edgar Buchanan (*Fred Lewis*); Emile Meyer (*Rufe Ryker*); Elisha Cook Jr. (*Frank Torrey*); Douglas Spencer (*Shipstead*); John Dierkes (*Morgan Ryker*); Ellen Corby (*Mrs. Torrey*); Paul McVey (*Grafton*); John Miller (*Atkey*); Edith Evanson (*Mrs. Shipstead*); Leonard Strong (*Ernie Wright*); Ray Spiker (*Johnson*); Janice Carroll (*Susan Lewis*); Martin Mason (*Ed Howells*); Helen Brown (*Mrs. Lewis*); Nancy Kulp (*Mrs. Howells*); Beverly Washburn (*Ruth Lewis*).

*The Film:* Completed nearly two years prior to release, *Shane* reflects the painstaking care characteristic of producer-director George Stevens, who had previously guided Jean Arthur through *The Talk of the Town* and *The More the Merrier*. Of the three, *Shane* would prove the legendary classic. Adding to its landmark status: this was not only Arthur's first full-length experience with the Technicolor cameras, but also her very last motion picture.

*Shane* owes its success to Stevens' detailed delineation of character and the interplay of human relationships, as well as his authentic approach to Americana. Arthur is a frontier wife who, while loyal to husband Van Heflin, is understandably drawn to Alan Ladd, the quiet, roving gunfighter who defends them against ruthless cattlemen before going on his way.

Loyal Griggs deservedly won an Oscar for his color cinematography, and the movie was warmly embraced by the critics. Because her role wasn't large, it's understandable that praise for the picture itself ("rich and dramatic") preceded the *New York Times'* Bosley Crowther's acknowledgment of Jean Arthur, whom he called "good as the homesteader's wife." But *Variety* paid her more detailed respect: "Miss Arthur gives the character her special brand of thesping skill, which shows through the singularly dowdy costuming and makeup." And *Photoplay*'s Janet Graves termed the actress "splendidly convincing as a pioneer woman."

# SELECTED BIBLIOGRAPHY

Berg, A. Scott. *Goldwyn*. New York: Alfred A. Knopf, 1989.

Black, Shirley Temple. *Child Star*. New York: McGraw-Hill publishing Co., 1988.

Capra, Frank. *The Name Above the Title*. New York: The Macmillan Co., 1971.

Carey, Gary. *Judy Holliday*. New York: Seaview Books, 1982.

Colman, Julia Benita. *Ronald Colman: A Very Private Person*. New York: William Morrow & Co., 1975.

Colombo, John Robert. *Popcorn in Paradise*. New York: Holt, Rinehart and Winston Co., 1980.

DeMille, Cecil B. *Autobiography of Cecil B. DeMille*. Englewood Cliffs, New Jersey. Prentice-Hall, 1959.

Dickens, Homer. *The Films of Gary Cooper*. New York: Citadel Press, 1970.

Druxman, Michael. *Make It Again, Sam!* New York: A.S. Barnes & Co., 1975

Eames, John D. *The Paramount Story*. New York: Crown Publishers, 1985

Easton, Carol. *Search for Sam Goldwyn*. New York: William Morrow & Co., 1976

Engstead, John. *Star Shots*. New York: E. P. Dutton, 1978

Fenin, George and Everson, William K. *The Western*. New York: Bonanza Books, 1962.

Fernett, Gene. *Poverty Row.* Satellite Beach, Florida: Coral Reef Publications, 1973.

Finch, Christopher. *Gone Hollywood.* Garden City, New York: Doubleday and Co., 1979.

Fontaine, Joan. *No Bed of Roses.* New York: William Morrow & Co., 1978.

Gordon, Max. *Max Gordon Presents.* New York: Bernard Geis Associates, 1963.

Green, Roger. *50 Years of Peter Pan.* London: Peter Davies, 1954.

Guiles, Fred Lawrence. *Hanging on in Paradise.* New York: McGraw-Hill Publishing Co., 1975.

Halliwell, Leslie. *Film-Goers' Book of Quotes.* New Rochelle, New York: Arlington House, 1973.

Hanson, Patricia King (executive editor). *The American Film Institute Catalog. Feature Films, 1931-1940.* Berkeley, California: University of California Press, 1993.

Hanson, Patricia King (executive editor). *The American Film Institute Catalog: Feature Films, 1941-1950.* Berkeley, California: University of California Press, 1999.

Harris, Warren G. *Cary Grant: A Touch of Elegance.* New York: Doubleday and Co., 1987.

Harvey, James. *Romantic Comedy*. New York: Alfred A. Knopf, 1987.

Hays, Will. *Memoirs.* New York: Doubleday and Co., 1955.

Higham, Charles. *Cecil B. DeMille.* New York: Charles Scribner's Sons, 1973.

Hirschhorn, Clive. *The Hollywood Musical.* New York: Crown Publishers, 1981.

Hirschhorn, Clive. *The Universal Story.* New York: Crown Publishers, 1983.

Jewell, Richard. *The R.K.O. Story*. New Rochelle, New York: Arlington House, 1982.

Kinnard, Roy. *Fifty Years of Serial Thrills*. Metuchen, New Jersey: The Scarecrow Press, 1983.

Kobal, John. *People Will Talk.* New York: Alfred A. Knopf, 1985.

Kobal, John. *Rita Hayworth.* New York: W.W. Norton and Co., 1977.

Lahue, Kalton C. *Bound and Gagged: The Story of the Silent Serials.* New York: Castle Books, 1968.

Larkin, Rochelle. *Hail Columbia.* New Rochelle, New York: Arlington House, 1975.

Lindsay, Cynthia. *Dear Boris.* New York: Alfred A. Knopf, 1975.

Logan, Joshua. *Josh.* New York: Delacorte Press, 1976.

McBride, Joseph. *Focus on Howard Hawks.* Englewood Cliffs, New Jersey: Prentice-Hall, 1972.

Martin, Mary. *My Heart Belongs.* New York: William Morrow & Co., 1976.

Merrill, Gary. *Bette, Rita and the Rest of My Life.* Augusta, Maine: Lance Tapley, Publisher, 1988.

Meyer, Susan E. *James Montgomery Flagg.* New York: Watson-Guptill Publications, 1974.

Michael, Paul (editor-in-chief). *The American Movies Reference Book.* New York: Galahad Books, 1969.

Munden, Kenneth W. (executive editor). *The American Film Institute Catalog: Feature Films 1921-1930.* New York: R.R. Bowker, 1971.

Oller, John. *Jean Arthur: The Actress Nobody Knew.* New York: Limelight Editions, 1997.

Parish, James Robert and Marill, Alvin H. *The Cinema of Edward G. Robinson.* New York: A.S. Barnes & Co., 1972.

Parish, James Robert and Stanke, Don. *The Debonairs*. New Rochelle, New York: Arlington House, 1975.

Parish, James Robert and Stanke, Don. *The All-Americans.* New Rochelle, New York: Arlington House, 1977.

Parish, James Robert and Stanke, Don. *The Glamour Girls.* New Rochelle, New York: Arlington House, 1975.

Parish, James Robert and Bowers, Ronald. *The MGM Stock Company.* New Rochelle, New York: Arlington House, 1974.

Peary, Danny. *Closeups, The Movie Star Book.* New York: Workman Publishing, 1978.

Photoplay Magazine. *Stars of the Photoplay*. Hollywood, California: Photoplay Magazine, 1930.

Pierce, Arthur and Swarthout, Douglas. *Jean Arthur: A Bio-Bibliography.* Westport, Connecticut: Greenwood Press, 1990.

Ringgold, Gene and Bodeen, DeWitt. *The Films of Cecil B. DeMille*. New York: Citadel Press, 1969.

Rivadue, Barry. *Mary Martin: A Bio-Bibliography*. Westport, Connecticut: Greenwood Press, 1991.

Robinson, Edward G. *All My Yesterdays.* New York: Hawthorne Books, 1973.

Rosen, Marjorie. *Popcorn Venus: Women, Movies and the American Dream.* New York: Coward, McCann & Geoghegan, 1973.

Ross, Lillian. *The Player.* New York: Simon & Schuster, 1962.

Russell, Rosalind. *Life is a Banquet.* New York: Random House, 1977.

Sarris, Andrew. *You Ain't Heard Nothin' Yet.* New York: Oxford University Press, 1998.

Schuster, Mel. *The Motion Picture Performer.* Metuchen, New Jersey: The Scarecrow Press, 1971.

Schuster, Mel. *The Motion Picture Performer, Supplement.* Metuchen, New Jersey: The Scarecrow Press, 1976.

Selznick, David O. *Memo From David O. Selznick.* New York: The Viking Press, 1972.

Sennett, Ted. *Lunatics and Lovers.* New Rochelle, New York: Arlington House, 1973.

Sennett, Ted. *Laughing in the Dark.* New York: St. Martin's Press, 1992.

Sikov, Edward K. *Screwball.* New York: Crown Publishers, 1989.

Spears, Jack. *Hollywood, The Golden Era.* New York: Castle Books, 1971.

Springer, John and Hamilton, Jack D. *They Had Faces Then.* Secaucus, New Jersey: Citadel Press, 1974.

Swindell, Larry. *Charles Boyer, The Reluctant Lover.* New York: Doubleday and Co., 1983.

Swindell, Larry. *Gary Cooper, The Last Hero.* New York: Doubleday and Co., 1980.

Swindell, Larry. *Body and Soul, The Life of John Garfield.* New York: Doubleday and Co., 1975.

Swindell, Larry. *Screwball, The Life of Carole Lombard.* New York: Doubleday and Co., 1973.

Thomas, Bob. *King Cohn.* New York: G.P. Putnam's Sons, 1967.

Walker, Alexander. *The Shattered Silents.* New York: William Morrow & Co., 1981.

Wray, Fay. *On the Other Hand.* New York: St. Martin's Press, 1989.

Zolotow, Maurice. *Shooting Star, a Biography of John Wayne*. New York: Simon & Schuster, 1974.

Zolotow, Maurice. *Billy Wilder in Hollywood*. New York: Simon & Schuster, 1977.

Zukor, Adolph, with Kramer, Dale. *The Public Is Never Wrong*. New York: G.P. Putnam's Sons, 1953.